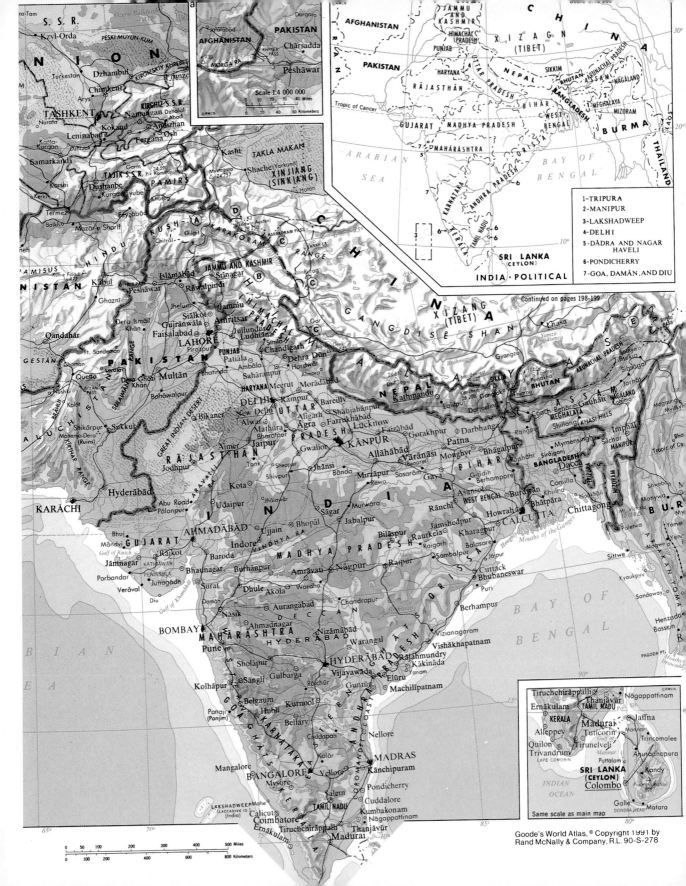

Continued on pages 198-199

1-TRIPURA
2-MANIPUR
3-LAKSHADWEEP
4-DELHI
5-DĀDRA AND NAGAR HAVELI
6-PONDICHERRY
7-GOA, DAMĀN, AND DIU

INDIA · POLITICAL

SRI LANKA (CEYLON)

PAKISTAN

Scale 1:4 000 000
0 10 20 30 40 Miles
0 20 40 60 Kilometers

Goode's World Atlas, © Copyright 1991 by
Rand McNally & Company, R.L. 90-S-278

0 50 100 200 300 400 500 Miles
0 100 200 400 600 800 Kilometers

Enchantment of the World

BURMA

By David K. Wright

Consultant for Burma: James F. Guyot, Ph.D., Professor of Political Science and
Public Administration, Baruch College, City University of New York

Consultant for Reading: Robert L. Hillerich, Ph.D., Visiting Professor,
University of South Florida; Consultant, Pinellas County Schools, Florida

CHILDRENS PRESS®
CHICAGO

A water cart passing ancient ruins of the city of Pagan

Library of Congress Cataloging-in-Publication Data

Wright, David K.
    Burma / by David K. Wright.
        p.   cm. — (Enchantment of the world)
    Includes index.
    Summary: An introduction to Burma, site of beautiful
and historic religious temples and land of constant
fighting.
    ISBN 0-516-02725-5
    1. Burma—Juvenile literature. [1. Burma.]
I. Title. II. Series.
DS528.5.W75 1991   90-21265
959.1—dc20   CIP
                                                      AC

Picture Acknowledgments
AP/Wide World Photos: 40 (left), 44 (top), 64
H. Armstrong Roberts: 106 (center right); © **Geopress,** 13
(right); © **E.R. Degginger,** 44 (bottom), 62 (right), 93 (left),
102, 106 (top left), 110; © **Koene,** 93 (right)
Historical Pictures Service, Chicago: 30 (bottom), 35
(2 photos)
North Wind Picture Archives: 32
© **Photri:** 5, 6 (top), 18 (left), 22, 26 (left), 30 (top), 36, 46
(right), 49 (left), 51, 53 (2 photos), 57, 68, 70, 85 (bottom
left), 88 (top), 89, 92 (2 photos), 94 (right), 101, 105

Reuters/Bettmann Newsphotos: 10, 11 (2 photos), 55, 58
(2 photos), 66
Root Resources: © **Alan G. Nelson,** 21 (left); © **Kenneth
W. Fink,** 23 (left); © **Art Petkiewicz,** 76 (left), 77 (2
photos), 94 (left), 99 (right), 106 (top right)
Tom Stack & Associates: © **Denise Tackett,** 20 (2 photos);
© **David M. Dennis,** 21 (right); © **Larry Tackett,** 76 (right),
106 (bottom center)
SuperStock International, Inc.: 26 (right), 47 (right), 78
(right), 80; © **Hubertus Kanus,** Cover, 16, 62 (left), 72, 75
(right); © **Peter Tsang,** 15 (right); © **Peter Schmid,** 47
(left), 88 (bottom); © **Giorgio Ricatto,** 49 (right), 78 (left),
84, 98; © **Von Knobloch,** 61; © **Ray Manley,** 74; © **Baldev
Kapoor,** 79 (right), 86 (left), 99 (left); © **Margaret
Sztojandovies,** 85 (top); © **D. Koblitz,** 86 (right); © **John
Baker,** 87; © **L.V. Kofod,** 96, 97; © **Suzanne Engelmann,**
104
Third Coast Stock Source: © **Zane Williams,** 91 (center),
106 (bottom left)
TSW-CLICK/Chicago: 6 (bottom), 9 (top), 75 (left), 91
(bottom), 107; © **Willie Stiven,** 4; © **Frank Folwell,** 9
(bottom), 12 (right), 46 (left), 79 (left), 91 (top), 103, 106
(bottom right); © **Anne Sager,** 24; © **Earl Young, 83;** © **Jack
Fields,** 85 (bottom right)
UPI/Bettmann Newsphotos: 13 (left), 39, 40 (right), 41
(2 photos), 42 (2 photos), 52
Valan: © **Christine Osborne,** 12 (left), 15 (left); © **Val &
Alan Wilkinson,** 18 (right); © **John Mitchell,** 23 (right)
Len W. Meents: Maps on 81, 87, 91
**Courtesy Flag Research Center, Winchester,
Massachusetts 01890:** Flag on back cover
Cover: In the Inner Court of Shwedagon Pagoda
                    Sanctuary, Rangoon, Burma

Children from the city of Pegu

TABLE OF CONTENTS

Above: The Irrawaddy River is one of the three important rivers in Burma. Right: Shoppers at a fresh produce market

Chapter 1

LAND OF CONTRASTS

Most Burmese follow the Buddhist religion. It teaches that good deeds, and especially good thoughts, are very important. Yet the Burmese have fought foreigners and each other since this land in Southeast Asia was first settled. Burma is one of the last countries to establish a television system. Yet the Burmese can buy cosmetics, rock 'n' roll cassette recordings, and other modern items smuggled in from abroad. Much of the countryside is fertile and the land is rich in natural resources. Yet food production and consumer goods fail to keep pace with a growing population of almost forty million people. The site of more beautiful, historic religious temples than almost anywhere on earth, Burma's homes and buildings are often in disrepair.

To complicate matters, there is no such thing as a typical Burmese person. The population is made up of many different ethnic groups. These people may seem alike to an outsider, but to a resident there are great differences. Religion, politics, life-styles, jobs, education, clothing—all offer clues to each person's heritage.

Burma is almost as big as Texas and is larger than Portugal and Spain combined. It is a mixture of religion and distrust, of ancient ways and the twentieth century, and of plenty and need.

GEOGRAPHY

Burma's neighbors include Bangladesh and India to the west, China to the north, and Laos and Thailand to the east. The Bay of Bengal and the Andaman Sea form the southern border. There are seven states and seven state-sized areas called divisions in an area of 261,218 square miles (676,552 square kilometers). The states are named after local ethnic groups: Chin, Kachin, Kawthule, Kayah, Mon, Arakan, and Shan. The seven divisions are dominated by people who speak Burmese and are called Burmese. These divisions are named after cities or geographical areas: Irrawaddy, Magwe, Mandalay, Pegu, Rangoon, Sagaing, and Tenasserim.

Burma is considered a tropical country. The northern tip is about as far north as Orlando, Florida. The southernmost point is as far south as Caracas, Venezuela. It is exactly halfway around the world from North America's east coast.

TOPOGRAPHY

Burma is the shape of a kite with a long tail of land between the Andaman Sea and Thailand. Much of the country is made up of mountains, river valleys, and plateaus. The mountains, valleys, and rivers run north and south, making travel east and west difficult. Burma is the home of the highest peak in Southeast Asia. Known as Hkakabo Razi, the mountain stands 19,296 feet (5,881 meters) in the far northwest. From the middle of the country south to the sea there is a huge, fertile, lowland area known for its rice production.

Rice fields in fertile lowlands (above) and Inle Lake (below) in the Shan Hills

Students protesting in 1988 carry Burma's flag, a student banner, and a photograph of Burma's national hero, Aung San.

BURMA TODAY

Not much world news came out of Burma until the spring of 1988. Buddhist monks and college students in the capital city of Rangoon, believing that their government was corrupt, staged huge protests. They were joined by people from all walks of life. After Ne Win, Burma's leader for twenty-six years, announced in July 1988 that he was stepping down, thousands confronted the military and were killed, injured, or imprisoned. In September soldiers took control of the country and used force to prevent further protests.

More than fifteen hundred Burmese were killed by the army during the 1988 summer. These rioters were angry at the government for many reasons. The country's economy was a total failure. Many ethnic groups wanted control over the part of Burma where they lived. And almost everyone was against

10

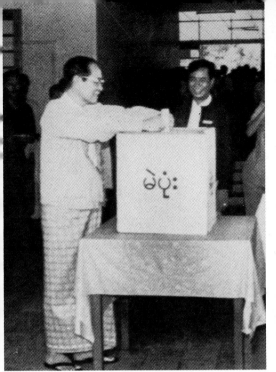

Left: General Saw Maung voting in May 1990
Right: A student stands next to a sign urging a boycott of the 1990 elections.

General Saw Maung, who took power on September 18, 1988. This old friend of Ne Win ordered the army to shoot protestors. Hundreds of people were killed. Thousands were jailed. In 1989 the government changed the country's name to the Union of Myanmar. By the spring of 1990 the army had forced an uneasy calm over the land. A restricted but competitive election was held in May 1990 and the party opposing the army's rule won by a landslide.

THE PEOPLE

Burmese have been fighting among themselves nonstop for more than forty years. The disagreements involve racial, political, social, religious, and language differences in a land where there are more than sixty different ethnic groups.

Burmans are in the majority nationwide. They are short, handsome people whose ancestors migrated into Burma from

Both men and women wear the traditional longyi.

Tibet long before history was written. There are more than twenty-seven million Burmans, which is 68 percent of the population. Most follow the Buddhist religion and live in the central lowlands, in river deltas near the sea, or in large cities. They are likely to be wet-rice farmers. Both male and female Burmans wear the *longyi,* a skirt that is knotted at the waist.

While the members of the ethnic majority are called Burmans, everyone who lives in Burma is called Burmese. There are many important minorities who are very different from the Burmans.

The Shans are mostly Buddhist people who are descended from persons who entered Burma from what is now Thailand. They number about three million, or 7 percent of the population. Their large state borders China, Laos, and Thailand in eastern Burma and is a land of hills and valleys. Shans are often rice farmers or traders. There are several Shan armies, all antigovernment, that

Despite ethnic backgrounds, all who live in Burma are called Burmese.

have staged hit-and-run warfare for years. In some cases these guerrilla fighters are led by *sawbwas*, traditional Shan princes. Other former princes have turned to education. Money for Shan weapons sometimes comes from smuggling and from growing poppies used to make illegal opium and heroin.

About 1.6 million Karens live in Burma. They make up about 4 percent of the population. The Karen state is next door to Thailand. These people move back and forth between the two countries. Hill-dwelling Karens practice slash-and-burn agriculture, which can destroy forests. Many welcomed Christianity that was introduced by the British. Others believe spirits affect their daily lives. Karens seldom grow the opium poppy but they do support guerrilla armies.

The Mons are a minority descended from ancient people who moved into Southeast Asia from China. Their language is different from Burmese, but they practice Buddhism. Mon art, architecture, and literature are highly regarded. There are about 1.5 million Mons in Burma today. Most are wet-rice farmers. Mon state, established in 1962, is between Rangoon division and Karen state in the southeast. Mon-speaking hill people, called Palaung, are found in small, fortified villages in the Shan state.

The Arakanese, who are Buddhist, Hindu, or Muslim, live in the western, seaside state of Arakan. The country of Bangladesh is their neighbor. They seem less rebellious than some other groups, but are just as independent. Some 1.5 million persons, or about 4 percent of all Burmese, are Arakanese. Burmans have traditionally mistrusted the Arakanese, many of whom are recent arrivals from the overcrowded nearby country of Bangladesh.

Fewer than one million Burmese are Kachins. They live in the northeast among even smaller ethnic groups and are famed as soldiers. Neither the British in the nineteenth century nor the Japanese in the twentieth century was able to conquer Kachin territory. Most Kachins follow a religion that views hunting and farming as spiritual activities. They also believe in the practice of witchcraft.

There are about 500,000 Chins in their state, which borders India. Most follow a traditional religion that includes animal sacrifice. The rest are Buddhist or Christian. They are good soldiers, too, having been recruited by the British when England ruled India. The Chins pay little attention to other ethnic groups, though they are very social with each other.

The Kayahs number only about 160,000. They also are known as the Red Karens and they have traditionally been governed by their own princes. Their tiny state, which borders Thailand, depends largely on smuggling goods into and out of Burma.

There are many other minorities. They include persons of Chinese, Indian, and British descent and such people as the fascinating Padaung tribe. Padaung adult females sometimes wear many metal rings around their necks, giving them the nickname

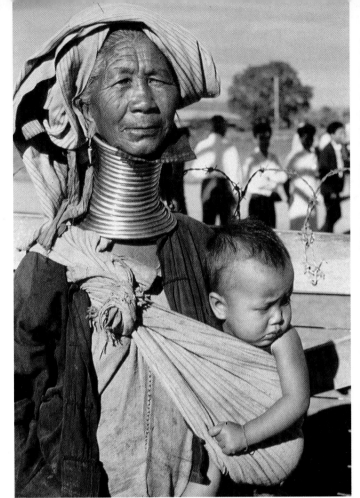

"Giraffe women" of the Padaung tribe

"giraffe women." There are other armies, such as the Burmese Communists and private drug-smuggling remnants from the Chinese Nationalists. The Nationalists were chased into Burma by the Chinese Communists in 1949.

Not all Chinese are rebels, of course. Many persons of Chinese descent can be found in Rangoon. Unlike the people who migrated into Burma from the north, these Chinese are descended from southeastern China residents who came to Rangoon years ago by sea. The urban young looked to China in the 1960s and caused unrest, but they have since kept to themselves.

All of these ethnic groups want to operate with their own set of laws. Few show any interest in a strong and united Burma.

Boats in the delta of the Irrawaddy River

Chapter 2

AN UNDEVELOPED LAND

THE LAND

Burma is very mountainous in the north and west. There is a huge plateau in the east. From this elevated semicircle, all of Burma slopes south toward the sea.

Major rivers begin in northern Burma or in southern China. They move south through deep gorges as thundering rapids, fed by cascades and by small, swift-running streams. The muddy rivers slow and widen as they flow toward the sea, eventually spreading into wide, completely flat deltas.

Three large rivers—the Irrawaddy, the Salween, and the Sittang—have been transportation routes for the Burmese for centuries. Their waters come from rain that has washed down from the hills and mountains. Rivers leave rich soil in the lowlands, pushing the muddy river deltas into the sea by as much as 1 foot (.3 meter) each year.

Because most of the country receives adequate rainfall, forests of bamboo and hardwoods, plus palm or pine, grow thickly at

Bamboo jungle (left) and a rubber plantation (right)

different locations and elevations. Burma is a major source of valuable hardwood such as teak. Hardwoods tend to grow where the weather is warm and damp. It is estimated that one tree of every nine in the country is a hardwood. Plantations of rubber trees, originally from South America, also thrive in the warm climate.

The world's largest bamboo trees, up to 1 foot (.3 meter) in diameter, are native to the country. Different varieties of bamboo are used for food, as building materials, and for everything from fishing poles to furniture. Sandalwood trees provide wood for furniture and an oil used to make perfume. Snarled, twisted mangrove trees grow to heights of 100 feet (30 meters) near the coast. They offer protection for animals and are cut for firewood.

Man's use of the land is most evident at lower elevations. Endless rice paddies stretch as far as the eye can see, from the coast halfway to China. In the central basin, north of the best rice-growing areas, farmers plant crops such as dry rice, corn, or millet. Burma was a world leader in exporting rice until 1965, when technology used in Thailand and elsewhere passed the country by. Since then hardwoods have been its leading export.

CLIMATE

Rain-bearing winds, called monsoons, sweep each year across Burma. These winds help create three seasons. The steaming rainy season, with a shower every day, occurs from May to October. From October to February each year, the land is cool and dry. Then March to May is the hot, dry season.

The coast and the mountains receive as much as 200 inches (500 centimeters) of rain a year. Rainfall gradually decreases northward to 20 to 40 inches (50.8 to 102 centimeters). The eastern plateau receives about 65 inches (165 centimeters) of rain annually. Monsoonal rains begin in the southern lowlands in May.

Snow falls in the mountains of the extreme north, yet temperatures where most people live are mild. This warmth is due in part to the mountains themselves—they keep frigid, Central Asia winds from penetrating into the lowlands. The average temperature in the capital, Rangoon, is eighty-one degrees Fahrenheit (twenty-seven degrees Celsius). Lowland temperatures do not range widely from one season to the next. Temperatures can exceed one hundred degrees Fahrenheit (about forty degrees Celsius) on the plains near Mandalay.

There is another force of nature that has left its mark on Burma: the earthquake. Down through the centuries, quakes have rocked different parts of the country in different years. The most recent major quakes took place in 1930 and 1975. Ancient temples swayed, cracked, or collapsed in the violent shudders.

Dragonfly (left) and newab butterflies (right)

ANIMALS

Tropical jungles teem with wildlife during the rainy season and shortly afterward. But as dry weather returns, fewer birds and animals are seen. Plants no longer offer protection because their leaves wither. Thick stands of vegetation become almost silent. All this happens because dry weather in the tropics is much like winter elsewhere: wildlife becomes inactive, dies off, or migrates.

Rainy-season citizens of the jungles include grouse, pheasants, parrots, peacocks, and wild fowl. Dozens of smaller birds are common. There are all kinds of insects, from dragonflies to mosquitoes to cockroaches. Frequently seen around forest streams—in wet weather or dry—are small clouds of orange, yellow, or blue-green butterflies.

If the Burmese have an unofficial mascot, it is the gecko. These tiny, silent lizards are found in every house and building and can

Peacock (left) and a gecko (above)

be seen running up a wall in search of an insect to devour. Geckos are harmless and go about their business under the approving eye of the country's landlords and homeowners.

Several annoying creatures, larger than mosquitoes, are everywhere during wet weather. Leeches are found underwater or on jungle leaves. These sightless beings can detect animal or human movement and cannot be felt, even when they attach themselves to a victim and suck their fill of blood. Scorpions offer good and bad news—they eat troublesome insects, but they can sting with their tilted tails, causing reactions that are sometimes fatal. Rats and mice eat many times their weight in food meant for humans and many carry dangerous diseases.

At the other end of the wildlife chain is the elephant. Wild elephants are common and so are their tame cousins who are trained to haul logs or perform other work. Elephants are built for

Some elephants are trained to be patient and reliable workers.

the tropics—they eat jungle growth, their hide is dry and tough, and their huge ears act as radiators, helping the large mammals get rid of body heat.

Adult Asian elephants weigh up to 8,000 pounds (3,629 kilograms), stand 8 feet (2.44 meters) high, and live as long as their masters—to the age of seventy-five. In fact, elephant handlers and their beasts have the same life cycles, so they work and grow old together. Elephants are intelligent and can work (at their own pace) for hour after hour. Ancient Burmese kings owned rare white elephants because they believed that one of Buddha's several lives was spent as such a beast. The beasts were pampered with luxurious food, daily baths, and their own homes.

Other large animals, including the rhinoceros, wild buffalo, bison, and deer, are scarce and must be protected. Also seen in higher elevations are bears, leopards, tigers and other wild cats, and gibbons and monkeys.

Poisonous snakes include pythons, cobras, and vipers, plus

A bengal tiger and a python

dozens of sea snakes found only in salt water. The dangerous Russell's viper is one of the few snakes on earth that will attack a human being without reason. Crocodiles make their homes in the river deltas, along with freshwater and sea turtles of all sizes.

Fish and other aquatic creatures are mainstays of the Burmese diet and are plentiful in streams, rice paddies, and in the ocean. Fish are harvested with nets instead of caught with rods and reels for sport. They can be as common as the freshwater European carp or the catfish or as exotic as huge and delicious saltwater tiger prawns (shrimp) or squid.

PLANT LIFE

The Burmese use plants in hundreds of ways. Since modern medicine is scarce, plants provide a means of fighting illness. As soon as a home is built, trees and shrubs are planted all around it. This vegetation keeps the home cool. It also provides food, since

A boy wears tanaka paste on his cheeks for protection from the sun.

the trees mature to bear bananas, mangoes, and coconuts.

Burma's most popular nonfood plant has to be the *tanaka*. Tanaka is made from a special tree. Branches are cut into lengths of less than 1 foot (.3 meter), then ground and mixed with water to make a lotion. The lotion dries to a powder, which is rubbed on faces all over the country. Tanaka powder feels cool on the skin and protects from sun, wind, and dust.

Much of Burma looks overgrown because the only ways to keep vegetation from growing are by paving, repeated walking, or animal grazing. Even villages with several hundred people appear as if they were built amid the jungle. Vines, creepers, and weeds grow rapidly during the rainy season.

NATURAL RESOURCES

Few countries have as many natural resources as Burma. Some have been mined or harvested for centuries. Others are almost untouched. Down through the years, nothing has attracted more attention than Burma's famous blood-red rubies. The best rubies are called pigeon blood. They leave the country in many ways.

Each year the government holds a ruby auction in Rangoon. Because the jewels are of average quality, only about half are sold. But a few blocks away, in a dimly lighted back room, a woman with $20 million in prize pigeon blood rubies secretly sells the stones for four times the price of diamonds. After the sale the buyer will smuggle the stones out of the country.

Rubies are mined at Mogok, in central Burma. Mining there is still done by hand. First a 10-foot (3-meter) hole is dug and a worker lowered into it. He or she scrapes the gravel bottom, finds some stones and sends them to the surface in a bucket. But the worker may overlook the best rubies, return at night to pick them up, and then sell them to an eager buyer.

The buyer, carrying a pack filled with the stones, usually hires someone or walks 200 miles (300 kilometers) east to the Thai border. There the buyer bribes border guards, crosses into Thailand near the village of Mae Sot, and then sells the rubies for large sums in Bangkok. Some buyers find rubies elsewhere in the country. Foreign visitors tell of trading half-used bottles of shampoo or old news magazines for uncut rubies and other precious stones.

There are other valuables from the earth. Jade is a pale green or white gemstone that has long been used in Oriental jewelry and carvings. Sapphires are deep blue stones, while emeralds are

Gold decorates the Sule Pagoda (left) in Rangoon.
A woman making baskets that are used to catch fish (right)

transparent green or yellow-green. Silver is mined in Burma and teamed with precious stones to make attractive jewelry. Gold is used to adorn Buddhist temples everywhere. Much of that flashy and expensive metal is imported from China. Jewelry is seen by the Burmese not as a luxury but as an important part of daily wear.

Other important natural resources include antimony, lead, tin, tungsten, and zinc. Iron ore has been found in several locations, but few sites are developed. There is plenty of petroleum and natural gas, but since Burma did not permit foreign companies to bring in modern equipment until recently, it now must import petroleum. Gypsum and limestone are plentiful and are used to make cement. The sea off Burma is filled with fish and has the potential to feed millions. Salt water also is the source of pearls created inside oyster shells. Pearl prices are high and rising.

Chapter 3

AN ANCIENT GATEWAY

Burma once was the gateway to Southeast Asia. In prehistoric times, people from the Himalaya mountains and from China moved east and south, down the country's river valleys and along the coast. They found a warm and fertile land where even earlier a few primitive people had lived in caves. The only signs left behind by the cave dwellers were stone tools. Scientists today believe some of these crude tools could be as much as five thousand years old.

The people who came from the mountains called themselves Pyus. They arrived in what is now Burma about two thousand years ago. Not long afterward, Indian and Chinese adventurers crossed Burma while trading between their two large nations. Some Indians migrated into what is now the Burmese state of Arakan. During these ancient times, persons living in Burma absorbed much of the cultures of India and China. Legends tell of an early visit by Siddhartha Gautama, who became the religious leader called Buddha, some five hundred years before the time of Christ. Despite such influences, the hundreds of Burmese tribes who adopted Buddhism never allowed their own culture to be forgotten.

THE FIRST BURMESE

The first people to leave extensive proof of their civilization were the Mons. They had come from southern China before recorded history. At first they settled in present-day Cambodia and in parts of Thailand. By the third century B.C., they were living in villages throughout what is now southeast Burma. The Mons were visited by Buddhist and Hindu sailors and traders from southern India. Like diners reading a menu, they chose only what they wanted of Indian culture and religion. Then they added their own beliefs and began to introduce their civilization throughout Southeast Asia. The Khmers, who are Mon descendants living in modern Cambodia, accepted Buddhism along with the Mon Burmese.

While the Mons populated lower Burma, another tribe living in what is now Tibet began to move south. These Tibeto-Burmans left their mountain homes because they were in danger of being overwhelmed by the governments of China and Tibet. So they braved brutal cold and thin air to cross Burma's northern ring of mountains. Once on the southern side of the Himalaya, they settled along the Irrawaddy River. They conquered and absorbed the Pyus. By about A.D. 100 these people, who are the ancestors of most modern Burmans, occupied much of northern and central Burma.

THE ENVY OF ASIA

A branch of these Tibeto-Burmans became the envy of Asia about this time. According to legend, they developed a civilization where there were no slaves, chains, or prisons—a kingdom where

men and women wore gold and jewelry and worshiped in Buddhist pagodas made of beautiful glazed brick. These artistic and progressive Burmans traded extensively with India and taught many smaller kingdoms how to run their governments.

Beginning in the sixth century A.D., the Mons were pushed south and Burmans took over cities. People from modern-day Thailand, called the Shan tribe, then marched into Burma. The stopping of the Shan Thais by the Burmans and the start of their capital city marked the rise of the modern-day Burmese. It also can be called the point where legends stop and history begins.

THE PAGAN DYNASTY

Wisely the first thing the Burmese built was a wall around their new capital city. The city, Pagan, was begun in A.D. 849. By the time its most famous king, Anawrahta, assumed the throne in 1044, the city was large and growing. King Anawrahta unified upper and lower Burma by conquering neighbors, then strangers. He was a brilliant soldier, using elephants to terrorize and overrun his enemies. But Anawrahta was religious too. He brought many captive Mons back to his capital city and they introduced wonderful religious art, crafts, and architecture. The king helped spread Theravada Buddhism throughout Southeast Asia. Pagan, filled with Buddhist scholars, became a vast construction site for temples and pagodas.

The Pagan Dynasty lasted until 1287. During that time, an incredible thirteen hundred monasteries, temples, and pagodas were built. The city was such an attraction to Buddhists that men and women came from great distances to devote their lives to temple building. Their religion taught that being involved in such

Remains of the Pagan Dynasty (above), which lasted until the Mongol armies of Kublai Khan (left) invaded in the thirteenth century.

projects would gain them merit in future lives. No slaves were needed for these beautiful and terribly ambitious projects.

MONGOL INVADERS

This kingdom withered when the Mongol armies of Kublai Khan invaded from China in the thirteenth century. The last king, Narathihapate, fled without defending his lovely capital. Mongol and other rulers kept the Burmese scattered and nervous by basing huge armies in Yunnan, the Chinese province next door to Burma.

THE TOUNGOO DYNASTY

Burmans settled along the large rivers between their ruined capital and the Andaman Sea. One city, Toungoo, began to expand along the Sittang River in the sixteenth century. So many Burmans sought refuge from the Mongols—and from warlike Shans and others—that this fortified town became powerful. The ruler, Tabinshwehti, conquered several southern Burmese cities and took control of the mouths of rivers. His invasion of Siam (now Thailand) failed, but Tabinshwehti was crowned king of all of Burma in 1546.

That really did not impress many tribes living in the country. The Mons gathered together in the southeast part of the country, from where they could stay in touch with the island of Ceylon (today called Sri Lanka). They wanted to preserve their form of religion called Theravada Buddhism, and Ceylonese Buddhists were famous for the way they interpreted the religion. The Mon capital of Pegu eventually became a center for the study of Buddhism, too.

*Vasco da Gama, the explorer who found
the sea route from Europe to Asia*

Other minorities were shrugging off Burmese influence. The
Shans and the Arakanese set up kingdoms on opposite sides of the
country, while several tribes living in southern China drifted in
and out of northern Burma. The country was breaking up into
many little areas, each with its own government, culture, and
heritage. Change would soon come from an unlikely source—
Portuguese sailors.

A PORTUGUESE KINGDOM

The Portuguese were great European explorers. Soon after
Columbus discovered America, Portugal's Vasco da Gama found
the sea route from Europe to India. Spices, gold, jewels, silk, and
other expensive items brought swarms of foreigners to the Far
East. One Portuguese sailor, Philip de Brito, became the customs
officer for a Burmese king at the port city of Syriam. This former
cabin boy schemed and tricked his way into power, then declared
himself king of lower Burma.

De Brito created a navy that kept the unhappy Burmese under
his power. Meanwhile he and his men looted Burmese temples,
stripping them of gold and jewels and shocking the religious
people in the area. In 1613 King Anaukhpethlun of Toungoo led
an army against de Brito's people and defeated them. De Brito was
captured and tortured to death for all to see. His Portuguese
followers were allowed to live but were exiled to central Burma.
A small tribe of people descended from these defeated Europeans
can be found today in rural Burma.

The Portuguese fled, but Europeans became common sights
along the coast in the 1600s. British, Dutch, and French trading
companies did a brisk business with the Burmese.

Chapter 4

WARS: LARGE AND
SMALL

The history of Burma is a history of many different people who
want to rule themselves. This is true today and it was true
hundreds of years ago. By about 1750 European interests were
backing different groups within the country. The Mons, supported
by the French, established a capital at Ava, near modern
Mandalay. They became Burma's defenders, chasing Indian and
Chinese marauders out of the country. But without warning,
Burmans under King Alaungpaya attacked and defeated the Mons.
This Burman military momentum continued until the entire
country was reunified.

ATTACKING THE THAIS

Burmese soldiers were so confident that they then attacked Siam
(modern Thailand). This aggression can be blamed in part on the
Thais themselves, since they had tried to convince Burmese ethnic
groups to rebel. The Thais were driven out of their own capital in
1767 and many of their best artists and thinkers were captured.
The talented Thais quickly influenced Burmese culture. In the
opposite direction, the Burmese took the western, seaside state of
Arakan next to India. Many Arakanese fled into British-controlled
India, vowing to recapture their homeland.

The Burmese must have been quite powerful. For example, the Chinese became concerned over Burmese expansion and attempted an invasion in 1766. Not only were they driven back, but invasions in the next few years by the Chinese were failures too. Burmese soldiers were equipped with spears, swords, crossbows, slings, and knives. They carried tough, woven shields for protection. Living off the land on their way to do battle, these thousands of foot soldiers must have been a dramatic sight as they approached their opponents across a dusty plain.

The rugged soldiers were no match for British technology however. The Arakanese sneaked into Burma from British India, attacking military outposts. Burmese soldiers chased the Arakanese back into India so often that they occupied small portions of Indian land. In 1819 Burma's King Bagyidaw was outraged when Indian nobility refused to attend the king's coronation. His troops barged into northeast India so boldly that, in 1824, war began.

THE FIRST ANGLO-BURMESE WAR

This First Anglo-Burmese War lasted two years—until 1826. It featured hordes of Burmese being mowed down by the cannon and rifle fire of British and Indian soldiers. Burma also found itself attacked by the Thais from the east. After heavy losses, the Burmese sued for peace. They gave Arakan to the British plus the part of India they had taken. The Burmese also lost the state of Tenasserim, next door to Thailand. The conflict cost Burma half its coastline.

Burma lacked leadership in the first half of the nineteenth century. This was so because Burmese kings frequently killed all

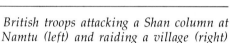
British troops attacking a Shan column at Namtu (left) and raiding a village (right)

potential heirs to the throne as soon as they were crowned. After the killing, the only people left to serve the king were the ignorant and those willing to follow their ruler without question. Europeans witnessed this and were shocked by it. The reports they sent back to their governments made British rule seem like a good thing.

THE SECOND ANGLO-BURMESE WAR

The Second Anglo-Burmese War, fought in 1852, cannot be blamed on the Burmese. The British looked at a map and saw that they could control the coast from Singapore to Calcutta by grabbing southern Burma. They also saw a brief war as protection—the Burmese were always making trouble along their borders. When two British sea captains complained that they had received unfair treatment in a Burmese court, the English had the excuse they needed. Following several British military victories,

The pagodas built for the Fifth Great Synod of Buddhism in Mandalay

the Burmese overthrew their weak king and installed a wise man, King Mindon, in 1853. He ruled over an inland area that is now central Burma.

Mindon was a traditional ruler. He served as the country's chief executive, obeying and enforcing ancient customs, which were the only laws. More important from the people's standpoint, the king served the Buddhist faith. Mindon was especially strong in religious matters. In 1861 he fulfilled one of Buddha's ancient prophecies by building the walled city of Mandalay. Despite his deeply held religious beliefs, he followed an ancient and frightening Burmese tradition: he buried fifty-two people alive under the gates and towers of his new city so that their spirits could protect the structures.

Mindon moved his throne to Mandalay and, in 1872, he held the Fifth Great Synod (worldwide meeting) of Buddhism. Evidence of this meeting can be seen today in the 729 pagodas, each holding a piece of Buddhist scripture, built for the occasion near Mandalay Hill. The scripture is so long that a book version contains thirty-eight volumes of four hundred pages each. The historic meeting ensured that the Buddhist religion remained free of outside influence, even though the country was later ruled by European Christians.

Burmese kings were smart to support Buddhism: it was virtually the only thing all Burmese had in common. A religious king was adored by the monks, who were also the country's schoolteachers. If a child grew up hearing great things about the ruler from the monks, he or she usually remained a loyal citizen.

THE THIRD ANGLO-BURMESE WAR

Thibaw, one of Mindon's sons, succeeded him. Thibaw was so worried about being overthrown that he forgot about supporting the religion. Instead, he ordered the deaths of thousands of his friends and advisors. The British heard about these atrocities and once again marched into Burma. The English also wanted to make sure that the Burmese weren't dealing with the French, who wanted to increase their trade with Burma. The British entered Mandalay without resistance in 1885. The Burmese had cooperated with the British because they believed the English would replace Thibaw and leave. But Burma henceforth was to be a part of British India. Thibaw, a weak man and an alcoholic, would be Burma's last king.

Making Burma a part of India was a very unpopular thing for the British to do. But they believed they knew what was best for colonial people. The Buddhist Burmese were quite unlike the Hindu or Muslim Indians. They also were unlike each other.

Today's borders were drawn by Englishmen who failed to notice important differences among the people they ruled.

Indians soon poured into Burma, seeking opportunity. They became shopkeepers, importers, moneylenders, and landowners. Indian and Chinese immigrants virtually took over Rangoon, working hard and frequently growing rich by exporting rice, teak, and other crops. The native Burmese resented the fact that foreigners were making money off their land. Burmese have never regarded Indian Hindus highly, because the Burmese believe in equality and Hindus support a caste system. Also, the British allowed several Burmese minority groups to govern themselves.

But the majority Burmans were not allowed their own leaders or a military or police force. They ran off to the hills as guerrilla fighters. Burmese army officers and politicians organized nationwide resistance. It took the British almost five years—until 1890—to subdue the Burmese.

THE YOUNG MEN'S BUDDHIST ASSOCIATION

Nevertheless, the urge to rule themselves continued into the twentieth century. The Young Men's Buddhist Association, made up mostly of Burmans, campaigned for independence. This nationwide group was led by Burmese who had been educated in England and elsewhere. They used the common link of Buddhism to rally the many different ethnic groups. This wasn't hard to do, since the British offended the Burmese by teaching that Buddhism was an inferior religion and by refusing to show respect for images of Buddha. To make matters worse, the British would not observe the centuries-old tradition of removing their shoes or boots upon entering a temple.

The Burma Road, built between 1937 and 1938, covered about seven hundred miles (eleven hundred kilometers), crossing mountains and passing through jungle.

The young Buddhists were especially strong at Rangoon University, where their association was called the All Burma Students Union. Students there staged a strike in 1936 that resulted in the British loosening their hold a bit. The following year, Burma was declared a crown colony and was separated from India. One of the leaders of the university's Young Men's Buddhist Association was a student named Aung San.

A TWENTIETH-CENTURY PATRIOT

Aung San dreamed of a reunified Burma, free of outside rule. He continued to create unrest among the Burmese while the British prepared to defend their colonies against the Japanese. Japanese soldiers had invaded China in 1937, and they were moving steadily toward Southeast Asia. The British built the Burma Road, from India to China, to provide the Chinese with weapons and supplies. Japanese military men knew that the road

Aung San (left) was the leader of the Burma Independence Army.
Japanese tanks pass an overturned British vehicle (right).

could create terrible problems for them. So they planned a huge
attack. In 1940 several of Aung San's friends were arrested to
prevent rebellions or cooperation with the Japanese. Aung San
fled Burma aboard a fishing boat.

The young Burmese made his way to Japan, where he was
arrested. The Japanese agreed to set Aung San free after he
promised to return to Burma and cause the British problems. In
March 1941 Aung San sneaked into Rangoon on a Japanese
freighter and quickly recruited thirty of his university friends.
They left the country and were taught guerrilla warfare by
Japanese soldiers. When the Japanese military invaded Burma in
December 1941, Aung San was the leader of the well-trained
soldiers who called themselves the Burma Independence Army.

Allied soldiers in Burma at the time included British, Indian,
Chinese, and American troops. The British and Indians were
pushed out of lower Burma. The Chinese and Americans were
then forced to retreat westward into India. Thousands of soldiers

British Royal Air Force bombers (left) pass over the Shwedagon Pagoda in 1941. After the Japanese had left Burma in 1944, the Burmese showed their loyalty to the Allies with posters such as the one above.

on both sides died in terrible jungle warfare. Burmese on both sides also perished in large numbers. The Japanese completed their conquest by June 1942.

THE BURMESE SWITCH SIDES

The Burma Independence Army grew to 10,000 troops. Most quickly saw that the Japanese did not care about them, but only wanted the Burmese to help fight the Allies. So when the British sneaked into Burma to fight behind Japanese lines, they had some support. Aung San and his troops officially joined the British in March 1945. World War II ended six months later with an estimated 100,000 deaths in Burma on all sides. More than four years of fighting had occurred under the worst conditions imaginable.

Aung San and his comrades from the university formed the Anti-Fascist People's Freedom League once Rangoon was regained

Prime Minister U Nu (left) and General Ne Win (right)

from the Japanese. The British created a cabinet that included
Aung San and completed talks in 1947 that would lead to
independence for Burma. Many ethnic groups agreed to cooperate,
but conservative and Communist Burmese broke away from Aung
San's party. Tragically, Aung San and several followers were
killed by gunmen who broke into a meeting in July 1947. Just
thirty-two years of age when he died, Aung San is still remembered
and respected today. Burma became an independent republic on
January 4, 1948, under a friend of Aung San's named U Nu.

The British had a profound affect on Burma and the Burmese.
These Europeans assumed that Burma was one country. On the
contrary, neither British India nor British Burma had ever
operated as a single nation until the English took control. British
authorities were sometimes kind to the natives but assumed that
English civilization was far superior to the civilization of Burma.
They let the locals know how they felt, which caused resentment
and feelings of inferiority. Burmese, told that they were descended

from people who were usually slaves, either believed the British and tried to take on British manners or became extremely anti-British.

Two things prevented programs after independence. First, the country had been badly battered by years of fighting during World War II. Second, different groups within the country began immediately to disagree violently with each other. Communist Burmese took to the hills, recruiting anyone who was dissatisfied with his or her place in society. The Karens started a rebellion, while Chinese nationalist troops entered Burma in 1949 after being chased from their homeland by Communist Chinese.

U Nu was a capable leader. He called his country the Union of Burma, keeping it neutral internationally and gaining the confidence of different Burmese while rebuilding the economy. However, in 1958, the Anti-Fascist People's Freedom League was split between U Nu and several of his former friends. U Nu asked the army chief of staff, General Ne Win, to become premier. Ne Win led a caretaker government, which held elections in 1960. U Nu won, but continued bickering with his rivals.

Fed up with conflict, Ne Win arrested U Nu and other government officials on March 2, 1962. He suspended human rights and constitutional laws, running the country with a council made up of military leaders. Ne Win's people ordered foreign business—and foreigners themselves—out of the country. They took control of banks and most businesses. Economic development stopped and then went into decline as a black market flourished.

In general elections in May 1990, the National League for Democracy won an overwhelming victory, but the top leaders were arrested and in December the National League for Democracy was outlawed by the government.

Above: A Buddhist monk collects donations in a market in Rangoon. Giving alms to a monk earns the donor merit in a future life. Below: Monks share a meal in Shwedagon Pagoda

Chapter 5

KEEPERS OF THE
BUDDHIST FAITH

This scene has taken place in Burma for nine hundred years. It is early morning, less than an hour after sunrise. A group of monks, called *pongyis*, each dressed in a saffron-colored robe and carrying a large lacquer pot, wanders through a Burmese village. Villagers, cooking their breakfasts, see the monks and run to the street with food. The villagers happily place rice, fruit, or various sauces in the bowls. They bow to the monks, thanking the religious men for the privilege of sharing. According to Buddhist teaching, the people gain merit in future lives by sharing with the monks. The people also prove their detachment from worldly goods by giving. The monks continue to gather food, since they do not eat after noon each day. Tomorrow, the scene will be repeated.

THE IMPORTANCE OF BUDDHIST MONKS

There are 113,000 Buddhist monks in Burma and about 700,000 boys or elderly, retired men who become monks for brief periods. They devote themselves to the study of the teachings of Buddha, which means "The Enlightened One." Monks must give up all

One young monk (left) uses an umbrella to keep
the sun off, as do the Buddhist nuns (right).

worldly goods when they don their dusty-orange robes. Besides
the three pieces that make up their robe, they are allowed to own
only a begging bowl, a strainer, a needle, a razor, and a mat for
sleeping. The strainer allows them to dip a stray insect out of their
drinking water, while the needle is necessary for robe mending.
Few monks wear shoes, but some carry umbrellas to protect
against tropical sun and monsoon rain.

Monks promise not to kill any living thing. They also pledge
themselves to poverty and to avoid relations with women.
Women are not allowed to touch a monk nor are they allowed to
give him anything directly. If a female has food to offer, she must
give it to a son, husband, or male bystander, who then hands it to
the monk. There are Buddhist nuns, but they are fewer in number
and are considered less important than the males.

Most males who remain monks into adulthood are monks for
the rest of their lives. They have given up worldly pleasures. In
fact, they have made more than two hundred promises concerning
poverty and sacrifice—all so that they can focus on their religion.

Left: Restoring a statue in Shwedagon Pagoda
Right: Young monks in school

They study and teach and perform tasks such as taking care of the local pagoda. Among their most important jobs is to guide every young Burmese boy as he learns about the faith.

AN ELABORATE CEREMONY

A Burmese boy's first exposure to his religion is an important one. Somewhere between the ages of nine and thirteen, a boy is readied for *shin-pyu*. This is the elaborate ceremony that takes place so the boy can become a monk. Once he is mature enough to correctly pronounce the ancient religious phrases clearly in the Indian language of Pali, he is dressed like a little prince in shiny silks and a golden crown. Neighbors paint his face with sunbursts of bright makeup. The boy is carried through the streets of his village, either on a wagon, a litter, or sitting high atop a car or truck. All the way from his home to the local monastery, the young man's feet do not touch the ground.

A huge feast, paid for by his family and attended by perhaps one hundred people, follows. After the meal, a monk spreads a sheet on the ground and the boy sits in the center of the sheet. The monk uses a traditional but sharp straight razor to shave off the child's hair and eyebrows. Later, the women in the boy's family will bury the sheet filled with hair near the pagoda. The boy must beg the chief monk, again in the ancient Indian language, to be admitted to study the scripture. The chief monk gives the boy his saffron robe and his begging bowl. Now he will act like and learn as a monk.

The young man remains a monk for at least a week. There is little hardship, since only part of the day is devoted to prayer, begging for food, and studying scripture. The rest of the time, the child plays games with other boys who have gone through their own ceremony at the same time he did. (Young and old monks alike sleep each night in the local *kyaung*, or monastery.)

The entire process usually takes place after the major harvest, since parents have some money left over to spend on the shin-pyu meal and ceremony. In contrast to the expensive shin-pyu, a girl goes through a simple ear-piercing ceremony. Both children are considered adults afterward.

Down through history, Burma has kept the Buddhist religion alive at times when other countries tried to wipe it out. Today Burmese Buddhism is unique—it is a blend of an ancient religion and the country's traditions, superstitions, and beliefs.

BUDDHISM'S BEGINNINGS

Buddhism came to Burma from nearby northern India. The faith began in the sixth century B.C. with an Indian prince, Siddhartha Gautama. Gautama was born into luxury. As a young man, he learned about suffering and death and this affected him greatly.

Images of Buddha are seen throughout Burma.

He walked away from great wealth, a huge palace, and his wife and family to search as a homeless wanderer for life's deepest meaning.

After many disappointments and depriving himself of food and comfort, he found peace and answers to his questions by meditating. Meditation was the path Gautama found to achieve enlightenment. He gained many followers because his teachings answered questions all people ask themselves. Buddha taught that a practicing Buddhist may not kill, steal, lie, commit adultery, or drink alcohol. Following certain rules and doing good deeds allows a Buddhist to be born as a better person in an endless cycle of birth and rebirth. The goal of all Buddhists is to reach *nirvana*, or salvation, free of endless rebirth.

Buddhism became India's official religion for a time. It is easy to see how the religion spread—the trade route from India to China passed through the heart of Burma. We can imagine Indian merchants explaining their religion and how it affected law, politics, and their lives as they traveled through a land that is almost as rugged today as it was thousands of years ago.

BUDDHISM'S EARLY ARRIVAL

Burma was the first country outside India to accept Buddhism. The stunning Shwedagon Pagoda, built about 480 B.C. outside of Rangoon, shows how early the religion was recognized. Since there are no regular religious services, pagodas serve to inspire Buddhists, helping them to meditate. This religion that focused inwardly did not become the country's major belief until the reign of King Anawrahta from A.D. 1057 to 1090. The king allowed his subjects to keep aspects of their primitive religions and blend them with the more thoughtful Buddhist teachings.

THE IMPORTANCE OF NATS

One of the most colorful things about the pre-Buddhist religions that continues in Burma today is the existence of *nats*. Burmese Buddhists believe that there are thirty-seven nats, or spirits, and that these spirits must be respected or bad things will happen. The nats are like Christian saints—they are called upon in time of need. Each (there are male and female nats) is a legendary or historical figure who died tragically.

Nats stand watch over virtually every temple and serve a deeply religious purpose, since worshipers cannot pray directly to Buddha. The spirits come in all shapes, sizes, and appearances and have names such as Lady Golden Sides or The Young Lord of the Swing. These names help the Burmese recall each nat's history. Likenesses of nats are most commonly found guarding temples as statues and in tiny houses created in the corner of Burmese homes. Each home also has a small shrine inside, where incense burns in front of red-and-gold symbols and gifts of fruit are

The spiritual home of the nats is Mount Popa.

offered. Nats, altars, and the sweet, smoldering smell of incense make this religion attractive to Buddhists and non-Buddhists alike.

The nats even figure in the country's geography. Their spiritual home is Mount Popa, a cone-shaped hill 4,980 feet (1,518 meters) high that rises above the central plain. The cone was created in 442 B.C. by volcanic ash left after Mount Popa erupted following an earthquake. Down through the years, the sudden appearance of the mountain seemed to make it a logical home for the thirty-seven restless spirits. Today, the hill is lush with vegetation, has temples and a monastery, and is a popular destination. The summit offers a great view of the flat countryside.

Indian Buddhism and Burmese tradition proved to be a good match. For example, Buddhists rejected Indian tradition that kings were given their thrones by one or more gods. Buddhists and Burmese have always thought that all men and women are born free and equal. Not even Buddha is viewed as a god. The

Politically active monks held a march in 1963 to protest the suppression of Buddhists in South Vietnam.

combination of faith and tradition sometimes made Burma a more peaceful and pleasant place to live than neighboring countries.

There are two kinds of Buddhism today—Hinayana (or Theravada) Buddhism and Mahayana Buddhism. The Burmese, along with residents of Cambodia, Sri Lanka, and Thailand, practice Theravada Buddhism. Persons living in Vietnam, China, Japan, and Korea are Mahayana Buddhists. Theravada Buddhists emphasize the value of pure thoughts and deeds.

Buddhism continues to be important today because monks frequently are politically active. They have a great influence over students, agreeing that the military government should treat all people equally and grant individual freedoms. Monks demonstrated—and were injured or arrested—during the 1988 uprisings in Rangoon and Mandalay.

OTHER RELIGIONS

Hinduism and Islam have large numbers of followers, particularly in the state of Arakan. Hindus came to India with

A Baptist church in Pegu (left) and a Chinese temple (right) in Maymyo

invaders from the north about 1500 B.C. There are an infinite number of gods and many large and small Hindu sects. What holds Hindus together is that they all believe their many gods represent one divine principle and life itself is one of those principles. Like Buddhism, which began later in India, Hinduism believes in an endless cycle of birth and rebirth, with good deeds leading to eventual escape from this cycle.

Followers of Islam believe in one god named Allah. Their god is the same as that worshiped by Christians. Muhammad was a prophet who delivered sacred books and told of one all-powerful creator of the universe. Followers are called Muslims. They pray five times every day facing Mecca, Saudi Arabia, where Muhammad once preached. The call to prayer, which booms out of loudspeakers at the Muslim mosque, is familiar to anyone who has ever been in an Islamic neighborhood.

Pockets of Christianity exist, created by Church of England and Baptist missionaries, among Burmans and hill tribes alike. The ancient Chinese Tao religion is practiced by some northern tribes. In many cases centuries-old religions are breaking down.

Chapter 6

GOVERNMENT AND

THE ECONOMY

On May 27, 1990, democracy won a great victory in Burma—or did it? An election few thought would ever take place produced a win for the National League of Democracy. This is a party whose leaders are in jail or confined to their homes by the ruling State Law and Order Restoration Council (SLORC). SLORC is a small group of military men who took over the government after the rioting in major cities in 1988.

These military men are led by Saw Maung, who appears to have no intention of giving any rights to the millions of people who turned out to vote for his enemies. The most visible of these enemies is a woman named Aung San Suu Kyi. She is the daughter of the martyred hero, Aung San, who tried to bring peace and a unified government to Burma following World War II. She is well educated, married to an Englishman who is a professor at Oxford. She is confined to her Rangoon home by government order. Whether Aung San Suu Kyi and her followers will be allowed to practice democracy in Burma remains to be seen.

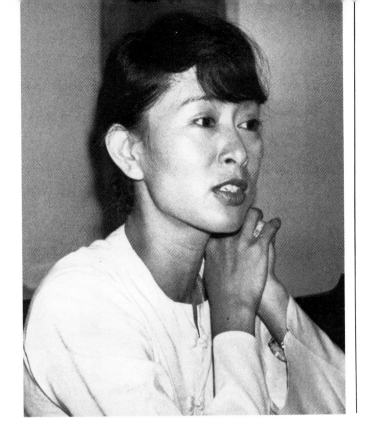

Aung San Suu Kyi organized the National League of Democracy to oust the junta rule.

Meanwhile, the government and the army are intensifying the war on "undesirable elements." This includes Buddhist monks, college students, and many minorities. The army has gone so far as to force minorities to carry supplies and ammunition as troops head into the hills. These civilian porters are even used as shields between warring forces. The government pays for its continued need for military hardware by selling the rights to harvest teak, or by such extreme means as selling most of the land around the Burmese Embassy in Tokyo, Japan.

In theory, Burma still has executive, legislative, and judicial branches. But SLORC runs the country. Fortunately, village politics has little to do with the national scene. Each village has a headman who is paid a small sum for collecting taxes. His job usually is inherited. The most powerful person in a village is the local monk or priest. That is true no matter what religion villagers follow.

Seven states and seven divisions make up the Republic of Burma. Each state or division is divided into townships. The townships are divided into either wards in urban areas or villages in rural areas. Government authority is weak in outlying areas and there are many large and small bands of armed guerrilla fighters. Even in urban areas, differences among the many ethnic groups sometimes cause problems.

Burma's judicial system is somewhat unique—a typical judge is an ordinary person who is elected to the position. This lack of training probably means that the same case could be judged very differently in different courts. But it also gives the impression that the ordinary person has a decent chance to be heard. These untrained judges rely on attorneys and law officers attached to the court to help them get through a case. Happily, law suits and other legal action are much less popular than in Western courts.

On the international scene, Burma has been completely neutral since becoming independent in 1948. The country under U Nu was one of the founders of the Nonaligned Movement, a historic strategy based on remaining neutral in international politics. Burma joined countries such as India, Kenya, and Yugoslavia in refusing to go along with either Communist or Western blocs of nations in the Cold War arms buildup that lasted from 1945 to 1990.

The country withdrew from the movement in 1979 because Burma feared that the group had lost sight of true neutrality. One advantage of neutrality is that the Burmese have managed to get along with both China and India, two huge neighbors that can be troublesome. The country is heavily in debt and receives aid from Japan, Germany, China, Czechoslovakia, and Thailand. The Japanese and the Thais have been criticized by the United States and others for supporting and trading heavily with the military government since 1988.

Because the country is so poor, public transportation is very shabby.

About 25 percent of total government spending is for the military. There are about 190,000 persons in uniform. Volunteers are fairly easy to get, since the country is poor and the military offers training and a job. Most money is spent on the army. The air force has several dozen fighter planes and a few transports. The navy's primary job is to protect coastal fisheries and to patrol the mouths of major rivers.

A DEFLATED ECONOMY

"The Burmese Way to Socialism" was practiced from 1962 to 1988. This form of government declared that any business or industry bigger than a "mom and pop" enterprise belonged to the people. Government leaders stopped importing virtually all foreign goods as a way to save money. So trucks and buses wore out, the people could not buy or replace sewing machines and other goods, and raw materials not found in Burma disappeared. The government limited gasoline to three gallons (eleven liters) per person per day. Progress came to a halt.

In the summer of 1988 student demonstrators (left) called for
the end to the one-party system of government and army troops
were used to guard government buildings (right).

A black market, selling illegal goods of every description,
quickly sprang up. Unable to buy necessities elsewhere, the
Burmese purchase everything from soap to cigarettes to toothpaste
from each other. Goods such as cassette tapes and portable
recorders are not officially imported. But tapes, recorders, and the
batteries that power them are readily available from black market
sources nationwide. The goods are smuggled into the country and
sold for wildly inflated sums.

This scorn for the government, combined with governmental
inefficiency, has prevented progress, despite low-cost loans from
other nations. Experts believe the economy of the country would
have collapsed by now but for the success of the black market.

The riots that resulted in death and repression in 1988 were
based on events in 1987. The government suddenly announced
one day that three pieces of currency, the 25, 35, and 75 *kyat* notes,
were worthless. People everywhere who had been saving the
paper money suddenly found that much of what little they had

was gone. Riots in Rangoon over elimination of the three highest pieces of currency shut schools and shops. Making the currency worthless was the government's way of trying to stop the rise of food prices.

The price of food was on the rise in 1987 because a rice shortage appeared certain. The bad harvest was due to a drought, but it was also due to government refusal to pay farmers decent prices for their crops. Unable to make any money on their rice, the farmers planted and harvested less of it. The country, once called "the rice basket of Asia," faced the first food shortages since World War II.

Inefficiency, decay, and neglect can be seen all over. In a market with no refrigeration, flies cling to meat and fish. Fewer and fewer public vehicles run each year, so there is more crowding. People ride on the roof and the bumpers of the vehicles that do run. In some parts of the country, the government's money is worthless. The currency there is bottles of whiskey or cartons of cigarettes, both smuggled in from abroad. There is only one telephone for every five hundred Burmese. Radios are common, but there are only about one thousand television sets in the entire country. Purchased on the black market, a TV set costs $4,000. There is only one television station, in Rangoon; it broadcasts a few hours each day.

Almost everyone must participate in the black market economy, since income is only about $200 per person per year. While Southeast Asian nations such as Thailand and Malaysia prosper, this resource-rich country slowly comes apart. Meanwhile, as darkness falls on the Burma-Thai border each evening, a few lone Thais or Burmese sneak precious gems out of Burma and consumer goods in. A couple of years ago, trucks with hardwoods and other goods roared in and out each night. But now, the government regulates traffic and makes sure taxes are collected. Thais, anxious to harvest teak, pay taxes to government officials and to rebels alike.

INDUSTRY AND AGRICULTURE

Mining and manufacturing employ about 1.5 million persons. Manfactured goods include processed food, textiles, petroleum, and natural gas. Some of the country's numerous rivers have been harnessed to produce electricity, but running wires to villages has been slow and there is a national shortage of light bulbs. Exported goods include teak and other hardwoods, base metals, edible seeds and beans, rubber, fish, and other agricultural products. Imported goods usually consist of machines needed for manufacturing, plus tools, spare parts, and raw materials.

Rice is by far the most important crop. It is grown in most parts of the country and is more important to the average Burmese than bread to the average North American. Rice in Burma is grown by 70 percent of the population, almost entirely without mechanical equipment.

GROWING RICE

To grow rice, fields are marked off by ridges of dirt about 6 inches (15 centimeters) high. In southern Burma, this takes place in April. The first monsoonal rains in mid-May soften the parched ground, with 1 to 4 inches (2.5 to 10 centimeters) of rain a day for two weeks. At the end of the month, farmers plow the fields into mud that is the consistency of cooked oatmeal.

Planting rice in the Irrawaddy Delta

    Meanwhile, seeds have been soaking in water, where they have sprouted tiny green shoots. These sprouts are sown in nursery beds and allowed to take hold for a few days. Then the beds are carefully flooded 1 or 2 inches (2.5 or 5 centimeters) deep in water. More water is added as the plants grow taller. By the middle of July, the plants are as much as 2 feet (.6 meter) high. They are plucked by hand and tied into bundles.

    Hand planting involves taking the stalks and sticking them into the mud. The field is then kept underwater throughout the rest of July and August. As the grain ripens and monsoon rains end, the fields dry out and the plants turn golden. The rice is cut in December and tied in bundles. It is dried in the sun and then carried to the threshing floor. Bullocks (steers) crush the chaff and leave the hardened grain whole. Farmers toss the rice and the chaff blows away, leaving the brown kernels until the husk is milled off.

    Recently in areas with adequate rainfall, more than one rice

Water buffalo are used as work animals on farms (left) and in the lumber industry (right).

crop a year has been produced. In contrast to this vast improvement in paddy land, many dryland hill farmers cause their land to deteriorate by practicing slash-and-burn agriculture. This involves cutting down large trees and burning the surrounding forest to clear the way for planting. This method causes topsoil to be washed away by rain and valuable vegetation must be replaced by hill tribes, which contributes to their poverty, mobility, and unrest.

Most farmers own the land immediately around their homes, where they raise vegetables. Popular garden items include chili peppers, onions, lemon grass (used to flavor food), various spices, squashes and gourds, potatoes, corn, beans and peas, tomatoes, and melons. Trees provide fruits and nuts, while many farms keep pigs and chickens and may have a pond that holds fish. Nonfood crops grown commercially include cotton for clothing and jute for rope. Harvesting teak, ironwood, and Andaman redwood is a way to earn a living for Burmese who live near tall forests.

Chapter 7

INSURGENTS, MINORITIES, AND DRUGS

Urban rioting—with more than one hundred deaths in a single day—and economic troubles in this unique country were shown on television and reported in newspapers everywhere in March 1988. But there is another antigovernment conflict going on in Burma, one that shows no sign of ending. It involves many minorities, international drug rings, and the country's military dictatorship. It is the world's longest guerrilla war.

THE LONG GUERRILLA WAR

Barefoot troops, carrying rifles and wearing parts of uniforms from different decades and different countries, lounge around a few shacks in a forest clearing. These boys and men and others like them in rural areas began the war in 1949. They were upset that the majority Burmans were given responsibility for the entire country after the British left. When they protested, Burmese armed forces attacked their villages. This made the minorities more

Karen guerrillas on patrol along the Thai-Burmese border in 1988

determined than ever to fight. For longer than many of them have been alive, their armies have conducted hit-and-run raids against government troops.

The Karens were the first ethnic group to fight. Over the years, others have joined the rebellion, although there was often no indication that the dozen or so active armies even talk to each other. Besides ethnic groups, there is a Burmese Communist army, various Socialist armies, tribal armies, and an army led by the world's most notorious heroin merchant. Some minorities, such as the Shans, have several different armies that use the Shan name but aren't close friends. Some guerrillas are sent money and arms from abroad by enemies of the government. They also raise funds by trading hardwood that travels illegally into Thailand. They impose their own "customs duty" on goods smuggled in and out of Burma.

Numerous Karen family members have fled across the border to avoid being caught in the fighting. The Karens who stayed behind found that Burmese army officials forced families to serve as porters. The army made women and children carry ammunition and supplies while hunting Karen men. Thailand leaves the refugees alone, preferring not to get involved in someone else's civil war. Refugee families frequently are supported by donations from church groups. The ragtag war shows no signs of letting up. And there is a darker side.

AN OPIUM WARLORD

The British introduced opium into Southeast Asia more than two hundred years ago. They traded the drug for spices, jewels, fine china, and other riches. When the English departed, thick fields of opium poppies, used to make deadly, addictive heroin, remained. People in many countries became addicted to opium and heroin. The poppies became a major crop for Burmese hill tribes to grow, because it made big money for them. Eastern Burma, northern Laos, and northern Thailand became known as the Golden Triangle of drug production. Until recently, no government had control of any of the remote hills or mountain valleys.

Into this untamed land came Khun Sa. He claims to be head of the Shan United army, but has more accurately been called the world's biggest heroin trafficker. For years, Khun Sa and his soldiers have bought the resin from the opium poppy, refined it into heroin, and distributed the white powder worldwide. These fifteen thousand armed men escort mule trains carrying drugs out of the Golden Triangle all year round. Loyal soldiers are paid well, but deserters and informers are tracked down and killed.

In recent years, Thailand and Laos have tried to convince their

Khun Sa smiles as reporters ask him questions during an interview in 1990 at his military base in the state of Shan.

people to stop growing the poppies. Free coffee beans, corn, and other seeds have been distributed and hill tribespeople who were addicted to opium have not been arrested. This has caused a decline in opium production in Thailand and Laos—but it has hiked prices in lawless eastern Burma. In 1989, Khun Sa's people harvested nearly 1,500 tons (1,360,800 kilograms) of opium, mostly in Burma. That is about 80 percent of all of the drug grown in the Golden Triangle.

Khun Sa told the United States in 1987 that he would stop exporting the drug if the United States paid him enough money and offered a crop-substitution program. American officials have vetoed the idea, feeling that the Burmese should take charge in their own country and that a payoff would not be wise. So the world's biggest heroin trafficker continues to operate. He and his people share responsibility for the crimes and deaths produced by heroin all over the globe.

VISITING A MINORITY PEOPLE

With its hodgepodge of humanity, Burma has no typical resident. For every city dweller, there is a remote hill tribesperson. For every farmer up to his or her knees in rice-paddy water, there is a farmer growing chili peppers, tobacco, or corn on dry land. And for every Buddhist, there is someone who either mixes Buddhism with an earlier religion, follows Islam, Hinduism, or Christianity, or believes in spirits that live in rocks and trees.

LIFE IN A KAREN VILLAGE

Only about 500,000 of the 1.6 million Burmese Karen live in the state named after them. The rest have moved into the lower Irrawaddy delta and other southern and southeast Burma locations. They all speak a Tibeto-Burman language similar to Burmese. Karen legends began far away in what may have been the Gobi Desert in central China. By the eighteenth century, so many Karens had wandered south into Burma that they spilled over into Thailand in search of unclaimed land. Other legends tell of a white younger brother who will come to free the Karen from poverty. That may be why early English missionaries were welcomed and why some Karen quickly accepted Christianity.

Today's Karen villages are isolated. They are made up of clusters of crude wooden houses with bamboo walls and thatch roofs built about 6 feet (2 meters) off the ground. There is no electricity and the only source of heat is charcoal from a small, central fireplace and from a partially open front porch where the food is cooked. Heat is needed to drive off the chill of a winter night spent where the altitude usually exceeds 2,000 feet

A Karen dwelling

(610 meters). There are one or two partitions inside the dwelling. Since many Karen are farmers, their pigs and chickens are sometimes penned beneath each house. After a meal, the leftovers are dumped between the floorboards for the animals. Competing for the food are a few dogs and cats who keep wild creatures out of the village.

Karen farmers take good care of their land, even though they clear it first by controlled burning. When preparing the soil for planting, weeds are chopped but the soil is not turned. Each field is used one year, then left fallow for up to twelve years. This method keeps the soil productive and so does maintaining numerous strips of virgin forest near the village. These strips help prevent erosion and, the farmers believe, ensure harmony with nature.

Crops grown include rice, chilies, sesame, tea, coffee, strawberries, peanuts, and beans. Because the Karen know how to care for the soil, they do not have to move very often. This allows them to grow tree crops such as bananas, coconuts, lichees, longans, mangoes, oranges, and peaches. The Karen tribe hardly ever grows the opium poppy. Some farmers train elephants to harvest logs, while others may keep a valuable animal such as a water buffalo. Surplus crops travel by pony or are carried by farmers and their families to the lowlands for sale.

Selling or trading crops are ways Karen farmers can bring extra food and other necessities to the village. Besides food they have grown, farmers may trade handicrafts, tasty bamboo shoots, or mushrooms recently gathered in the forest. Currency is not in complete use, so bartering is normal. Farmers return from trading in a lowland market town with salt, iron, ammunition, kerosene, utensils, blankets, cloth, medicine, needles, thread, or inexpensive jewelry. They will then trade some of the lowland material for a bit of other villagers' homegrown surplus.

CLOTHING AS ART

Karen women are famous for their ability to weave cloth. Men, women, and children all wear blouses made of handwoven cloth, usually cotton. The cotton is a riot of color, adorned with embroidery that may even feature tiny seeds as part of the design. Girls and young women wear a long version of this garment, starting with a simple white that carries more and more designs as the wearer learns the art of sewing. Men and women both wear cloth turbans.

Beads, bracelets, earrings, and jewelry also are of high quality. Karen women wear bracelets by the dozens, made of hammered aluminum, brass, copper, or silver. Beads in hundreds of varieties are worn by young girls and women, while some Karen bachelors

A Karen mother and her children

wear a single bead choker and sometimes keep their hair in a long braid combed to the side. Earrings, worn by females, are usually silver. Men and women, but especially men, adorn their arms, legs, chests, and backs with tattoos.

The most important person in each village is the priest. He is so vital that his death often results in the village site being abandoned for another. Priests set dates for ceremonies and celebrations and watch the morals of villagers. The priest must please any offended spirits or else the crops will fail and villagers will starve. Other duties include dividing up farmland and deciding who is right in a dispute between neighbors. Even villages that call themselves Christian are concerned with the priest and how he deals with the spirit world.

Chapter 8

CULTURE—ELEGANT, INNOCENT, UNSPOILED

The ultimate examples of Burmese culture are found throughout the country in thousands of pagodas and temples.

THE BEAUTY OF RELIGIOUS BUILDINGS

The importance of centuries of religious architecture is visible everywhere in Burma. Graceful towers point toward the sky in towns and villages and in the open country. In temples there are hundreds of statues of Buddha. On the walls and ceilings are paintings that are likenesses of Buddha.

A *stupa*, or bell-shaped monument in a temple complex, is a solid structure with a small chamber inside. In this chamber a relic (such as a lock of hair or piece of bone) from the Buddha is kept. Sometimes sacred texts are enshrined in a stupa. Buddhists meditate while walking clockwise around the outside of a stupa.

Stupas in the inner court of Shwedagon Pagoda

Pagodas, old and new, are typically constructed of brick and are usually painted white and covered with genuine gold. Burma's best example of a classic pagoda is Shwedagon in Rangoon. With one massive, main stupa and dozens of smaller shrines, the pagoda glistens in the sun "like a sudden hope in the dark night of the soul," according to an English writer.

FOR EVERY PAGODA, A LEGEND

Like many famous sites in Burma, there is a legend connected with the Shwedagon pagoda. About the time the Buddha was a young man, there lived in lower Burma a king named Okkalapa. The king owned a hill where relics from three earlier Buddhas were kept. He hoped that another Buddha would visit and renew the importance of the relics. Buddha appeared to the king in a vision, saying he, too, would meditate over the relics. As Buddha meditated in northern India, two traveling traders from lower Burma offered him cake. He showed his gratitude by giving them eight hairs from his head.

The traders were robbed of two hairs by an Indian prince. Two more of the hairs were taken by a pirate as the travelers crossed the Bay of Bengal. But they met King Okkalapa with four hairs still in their possession. The king had a feast that included native gods and nats. They all decided to erect a stupa to enshrine their own Buddha relics and the hairs from Buddha.

When the king opened the box containing the four hairs, they had become eight once again. Even more dramatic, they gave off a brilliant light that radiated to all corners of the earth. The crippled, blind, and deaf who were touched by the rays of light could walk, see, and hear once again. There was an earthquake, a

The central stupa of Shwedagon is covered with precious stones and slabs of gold.

thunderstorm of precious gems, and trees bore fruit instantly. A sixty-six-foot (twenty-meter) stupa was built for the relics. Smaller pagodas of brick, tin, and marble also were created.

BURMA'S MOST FAMOUS PAGODA

The Shwedagon pagoda today has a central stupa that rises 325 feet (99 meters) above the city. It is plated with almost 8,700 slabs of solid gold. The tip of the stupa has 5,448 diamonds and 2,317 rubies, sapphires, and topaz. A huge emerald at the very top catches the first and last rays of the sun. All of these jewels sit above a metal *hti*, or umbrella, that is more than 30 feet (9 meters) high. The umbrella has nearly 1,500 gold and silver bells that ring sweetly as the breezes blow. Huge bells nearer the ground, one weighing 40 tons (36,288 kilograms), are rung by Buddhists as a

*The Ananda Temple in Pagan (left) and the Sacred Pagoda Boat,
the "Karaweik Barge," on Inle Lake (right) are two of the
many religious sites in Burma.*

way to share the good deeds they have done. Visitors to Burma
with no exposure at all to Buddhism are deeply moved by
Shwedagon. Neither time, weather, war, nor earthquake has
destroyed its eight sides and sixty-four stupas. The gold and
jewels that adorn the landmark are said to be worth $750 million.

There are so many magnificent temples throughout the country
that a visitor is almost never out of sight of one, old or new. Each
seems to have its own particular legend. This is especially true at
Pagan in central Burma. This ruined city has thousands of
pagodas and temples created across a broad plain by a series of
kings. Conflicts, earthquakes, and the passing of time have taken
their toll on these wonderful buildings, which aren't carefully
maintained because there is more merit to building a pagoda or
temple than keeping one up. Nevertheless, Burma's temple
architecture and pagoda designs are world famous.

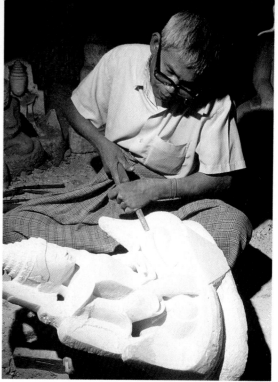

Burmese girls wearing longyis *(above)
and a craftsman carving an image
of Buddha in marble (right)*

ARTS AND CRAFTS

There are many Burmese crafts: bronze and brass sculpture, embroidery, furniture, jewelry, knitwear, lacquerware, marble sculpture, metalwork, umbrellas, weaving, woodcarving—the list seems endless. Crafts fall into three broad categories: the finished product either has religious importance, is wearable, or is in frequent use around the house.

Lacquerware originated in China. In Burma today, raw lac is tapped from a special tree. Since it turns hard and black when it hits the air, the substance is quickly spread over a bamboo bowl or box. The surface is then polished to a black, mirror finish, followed by engraving or painting. Multicolored lacquer products take months to produce. Vases, jewelry boxes, and dinnerware are available in this unique product.

Burmese women, whether they are Burman, Shan, or Mon, excel in embroidery, sewing, and weaving. Cotton or silk are commonly

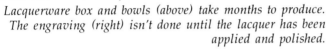
Lacquerware box and bowls (above) take months to produce. The engraving (right) isn't done until the lacquer has been applied and polished.

used fabric. Besides producing clothing unique to their ethnic background, they make handbags and wall hangings that are known round the world. Since jewelry is considered part of a Burmese woman's wardrobe, she is likely to buy Burmese jewelry products with the money she makes with her loom. Hill tribe females are often seen with dozens of bracelets, earrings the size of tea cups, and neck rings that weigh several pounds.

Gold leaf, paper-thin pieces of real gold, is turned out in huge quantities. That is because the Burmese paste the leaves on images of the Buddha in temples all over the land. Gold nuggets from northern Burma are pounded, then pressed until they are so thin as to be almost transparent. They are carefully packaged in oily paper and are slightly smaller—and much thinner—than a playing card. Gold leaf has been stuck on some images so thickly that the image looks like a shapeless blob and is worth thousands of dollars.

Seen as often as gold are wood carvings. These adorn roofs,

A chinthe *guarding Shwedagon Pagoda (left) and furniture (right) are carved from wood.*

walls, doors, and windows of pagodas and monasteries. The figures are likely to be nats or *chinthes,* lionlike figures created to guard religious sites. Pottery is everywhere too. It is especially important, since the Burmese store all kinds of food in huge pots. Almost as common are bells of all sizes, heard in every pagoda.

BURMESE THEATER

There aren't many famous novels by Burmese writers. Nor are there great plays or poems. Instead, the Burmese have combined drama, dance, and music to create *pwes,* different forms of theater seen at festivals. A pwe is performed for hours on a portable stage and can include dancers, puppets, poets, mimes, comedians, actors, and musicians. The action usually is accompanied by a traditional Burmese band, playing drum, gong, and cymbal music unlike anything heard in the Western Hemisphere. Occasionally harps or flutes are played by individual musicians.

A traditional dancer (left) and a musician playing a kyay-waing, *or gong-circle (right)*

Pwe stories have been handed down through generations. Many are descended from the Hindu *Ramayana*, an epic that tells how a prince named Rama recovers his kidnapped wife from evil forces. Themes not related to this epic usually tell of one of the many lives of the Buddha that led to his reaching nirvana. In parts of the country, it is considered bad taste for a human to portray the Buddha. So puppets are used instead. Puppeteers move their strings and create dozens of voices to keep the crowd involved.

Often seen on the pwe stage are dancers. They bend and move at unusual angles, copying steps and actions that were brought to Burma by Thai dancers hundreds of years ago. Frequently masked, the dancers perform the same religion-based moves that kept Burmese kings hypnotized with their beauty. Dance troupes, dressed in vivid costumes, are active all over the country. Burma's National Theater dance troupe has traveled worldwide, performing before presidents, prime ministers, and royalty.

The Supreme Court Building in Rangoon

Chapter 9

CITIES LARGE

AND SMALL

Burma is a country of thousands of villages. If it weren't for the vegetation, a hiker could walk from the southern seashore to the Himalaya foothills and probably never lose sight of at least one Burmese village. Cities will increase in importance as the growing population causes them to swell.

THE NATION'S CAPITAL

Rangoon, called Yangon, is the seat of government. With about 2.5 million residents, it is also the nation's largest city. Rangoon is five times the size of any other city in the country, but it remains smaller than other cities in the area, such as Calcutta in India or Bangkok, the capital of Thailand.

Rangoon's history can be traced back more than two thousand years, to the early stages of Buddhism. The hill where the suburban Shwedagon Pagoda now stands attracted Buddhists, in part because it could be seen for some distance. Where better to build a monument to the faith?

The city has always guarded the entrance to the Irrawaddy River, and it has been a major site for civilizations such as the Mons. But its most important reason for existing has been religious. Early European visitors who sailed up the river reported being overwhelmed by the sight of the incredible pagoda gleaming in the distance.

Despite European influence, it was a Burman king, Alaungpaya, who captured a Mon village near the pagoda in 1755. He renamed the village Yangon, or safe place, which came to be pronounced Rangoon by foreigners. As other ports, such as Syriam, rose and fell, Rangoon grew. The British occupied the city, but they were hard on it. A fire nearly destroyed everything in 1841, while the Second Anglo-Burmese War in 1852 wiped out fortifications and damaged many buildings, resulting in numerous civilian deaths. Evolving into a major trading center, the city became the nation's capital about one hundred years ago.

British and Burmese alike were optimistic about Rangoon. It was the site of the nation's foremost college and had wide, tree-lined streets with modern architecture. Just as important, huge amounts of agricultural commodities were floated down the Irrawaddy in huge amounts for export. Row upon row of riverside warehouses promised a bright future. Sadly, history got in the way.

The British mistreated the Burmese by trying to convince the Asians that European life was superior. This caused so much resentment among educated Burmese that students hated the very school system that had taught them so much. These students watched the Japanese push Britain out of Burma in World War II and realized that no civilization was superior to any other. When Englishmen returned to Rangoon in 1946, they knew they had to

Rangoon is the largest and busiest city in Burma.

give up not only India, but Burma as well. Independence, in 1948, proved to be good for the Burmese and bad for the city of Rangoon.

Burmese government officials were handed a lovely, well-planned city that needed a lot of maintenance in the tough tropical climate. In attempting to build a nation, repairs to streets, plumbing, buses, and buildings were neglected. That neglect began in the 1940s and it shows. A series of inefficient governments has made the problem worse.

Today's Rangoon is in a state of quiet decay. Chunks of pavement are missing, mildew covers buildings, plaster peels from ceilings, and the smell of sewage is everywhere. Balconies dangle and pieces of stucco are gone from buildings. The water is extremely hazardous to human health. The city is ringed by shantytowns and the once-prosperous river warehouses are

Maha Bandoola Street

ramshackle. There is a permanent shortage of spare parts for virtually every machine, and electricity and telephone services are not dependable. Many everyday goods, such as charcoal for cooking fuel and gasoline, are scarce and must be rationed. The wet season brings mud, insects, snakes, and lizards. In the dry season, the evening skies can be thick with bats.

SOUTHEAST ASIA'S MOST CHARMING CITY

Yet for all of its problems, Rangoon may be the most charming city in Southeast Asia. All streets — the wide avenues and the dark alleyways — are safe for pedestrians day or night. Shops and markets display an incredible variety of old and new items that no one has seen anywhere else since colonial days. Rangoon's citizens, many of whom are of Indian or Chinese descent, are busy, friendly, and fascinating to watch. Craftsmen make spare

Central Rangoon has wide avenues (above),
and is the site of the main post office (below
left) and Independence Monument (below right).

Traffic in central Rangoon (above);
a corner candy and tobacco stand (right)

parts out of other spare parts, patching together items that should
have been junked years before.

Without many vehicles, the air is clean, even if it does not
always smell good. There are, of course, several pagodas of
historical importance. About the only frightening things are the
large numbers of police and military personnel and rolls of barbed
wire. All are left over from past rioting.

Outside the downtown area are two large, man-made lakes,
zoological gardens, and Rangoon University. The black market is
obvious everywhere, with people selling everything from foreign
cigarettes to bootleg cassette tapes at any busy intersection. Traffic
is a mixture of large and ancient trucks and buses, new Japanese
pickup trucks, 1950s English and American cars, plus bicycles.
Since it is warm most of the year, residents of this metropolitan
area tend to wait for the cool of evening to shop and dine. In all,
Rangoon is a city where time has stood still since 1948.

The remains of the royal palace of King Mindon in Mandalay

THE ROAD TO MANDALAY

Mandalay, Burma's second-largest city, is about 350 miles (563 kilometers) due north of Rangoon. It, too, is on the Irrawaddy River. Mandalay is much smaller, with a population of only about 460,000. History here is measured in years, not centuries, since the city did not exist before 1857. It was built under the reign of King Mindon, who wanted to restore importance to the vast plain of central Burma. Mindon looked down from atop Mandalay Hill and ordered construction below after consulting monks and prophets.

A religious man, Mindon built a gigantic, walled royal palace, held conferences, and began a state-supported fine arts school. At his death, he was succeeded by his son, Thibaw. Thibaw and his queen were lazy and failed to defend the huge teak palace during the final Anglo-Burmese War in 1885. The palace became an

*Above: The pace of life slows down in Mandalay, with less traffic and
pony carts sometimes used for transportation. Mandalay Hill (above) is about
an hour's climb. Below: Shopping in Mandalay's open market*

A dock worker on the Irrawaddy River

English fort and the City of Gems, as Mandalay was called, prospered. In 1942 the British hastily departed and the Japanese used the city as their northern headquarters. Sadly, the wooden palace was destroyed in 1945 when British and Indian troops retook the city in vicious fighting. Despite the destruction, palace walls still dominate city streets.

Today, Mandalay is reached from Rangoon in a day by train, car, or bus, or in an hour by plane. The pace is so slow in the city itself that pony carts are a common form of transportation. They take visitors to artists' workshops where gold leaf, ivory, tapestry, silk weaving, and other skills are the best in the country. Mandalay Hill is about an hour's climb. It is a popular spot for devout Buddhists and for others who want a great view of the city, the river, and the plains.

Just south of Mandalay are the sites of two ancient royal cities—Amarapura and Ava. Back in the city itself, there are numerous magnificent temples and pagodas, resplendent in gold. The smell of fish mixed with diesel oil is a reminder of that huge "liquid highway," the Irrawaddy River, just to the west of the downtown area.

BURMA'S OTHER CITIES

There is no accurate way to tell how many people are in most other Burmese cities. The last countrywide census was taken in 1983 and since then populations have changed somewhat in some places and totally in others.

Moulmein is Burma's third-largest city. It is approximately 70 miles (113 kilometers) east of Rangoon. Despite its proximity to the capital, it is often off limits to foreigners. The Burmese point out that this city at the mouth of the Salween River is a popular hangout for smugglers, since it is near the Thai border and therefore may be dangerous. Actually the city is very tropical, with palm trees and pastel, wooden houses. Perhaps because of the smugglers, Moulmein seems more lively than most Burmese towns. It has an ancient and romantic promenade along the river and, some miles to the south, the small beach town of Amherst.

Bassein is a large town in the Irrawaddy River delta. Its products include rice, jute, and large and sturdy pottery. Dotted with pagodas, it is the site where hundreds of sea turtles lay thousands of eggs for a few weeks each year. Like every other Burmese city, men and women wear longyis and smoke *cheroots*, large, green home-rolled cigars as big as sausages. The markets look the same, too—run-down but occasionally bustling and selling every conceivable fruit, vegetable, bird, and fish known to man.

Pegu is the former Mon kingdom fifty miles (eighty kilometers) northeast of Rangoon. It is the jumping-off point for the golden rock of Kyaik-Tyo. This huge, gold-painted boulder is perched precariously on the very edge of a cliff. A small pagoda, said to contain one of the Buddha's hairs, sits atop it. Back in Pegu is a

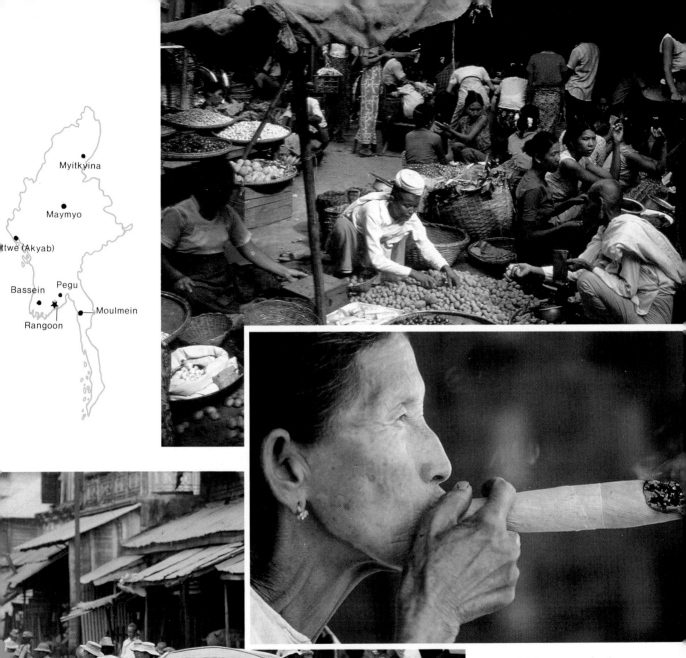

A market in Pagan (top), a woman smoking a cheroot (above), and a bustling street in Pegu (left)

Myitkyina

Maymyo

ttwe (Akyab)

Bassein

Pegu

Rangoon

Moulmein

Because of its altitude and cooler climate, Maymyo once was a retreat for English families. Quaint stagecoaches are used as taxis.

pagoda almost as tall as the Shwedagon in Rangoon. There is also a huge Allied cemetery nearby—a reminder of the dreadful conflict that flashed across Burma in World War II.

The hill town of Maymyo east of Mandalay once was a retreat for English families when the heat on the plains drove temperatures past 100 degrees Fahrenheit (38 degrees Celsius). At an elevation of 3,300 feet (1,006 meters), the climate is pleasant and cool enough for pine trees to grow. There are sturdy, English-built brick cottages (rarities in Burma), horse-drawn carriages, waterfalls, and a botanical garden. The town is of little importance today except to fans of colonial history.

Akyab, also known as Sittwe, is in the far southwest and was built on an island on the Bay of Bengal. Many Muslims and Hindus live here. Akyab has a prosperous fishing industry, Victorian houses, crafts more common to Bangladesh than to Burma, and a beautiful and empty stretch of beach. Like most other cities any distance from Rangoon, it is usually out of bounds to tourists.

Homes along the edge of Inle Lake are built on stilts (left).
A taxi boat traffic jam leading to the lake (right)

Burma's northernmost town of any size, Myitkyina has probably not seen any Westerners in years. This city is in the foothills of the Himalaya. It is a center for area tribes that worship forest spirits. They gather to hold a spirit festival here each January. Because of its nearness to the northern border, there is a strong Chinese flavor to the remote area.

INLE LAKE

Inle Lake, southwest of Mandalay in the Shan Hills, is famous the world over for the way its residents row their boats. The lake is long and narrow but very shallow, with lots of weeds and other growth just beneath the surface. So boatmen stand to look for submerged problems. They stand at the stern of their small craft and push them along with both arms—and one leg—wrapped around the oar. As awkward as the method looks, it works for these people.

Left: The unique rowing method used by boatmen on Inle Lake   Above: Bird's Nest Islands, part of Merqui Archipelago

Fishermen in this unusually clear water have for years used cone-shaped nets to trap fish. Even more unusual, the people who live around the lake toss topsoil on lake vegetation to create floating gardens. These gardens can be towed by boats if moving becomes necessary, or sold if the family decides to give up planting. Houses are built over the water on short stilts and shopping takes place at floating gardens, as numerous boats filled with goods of all sorts meet at prearranged places and times. Several old English resorts look down on the lake from the very green hills on either side of this unique body of water.

In contrast to this lush, fresh water are the islands far to the south in the Mergui Archipelago. These islands are the homes of modern-day pirates, people of mixed descent who prey upon unsuspecting boats that sail up this coast from Malaysia and Thailand. The islands and outcroppings provide hiding places for these sea robbers, who will continue to obey only their own laws as long as the Burmese are unable to control the country.

Chapter 10

LIFE'S ROUTINE

Burma is one of the poorest countries on earth. Yet Burmese are as eager to learn as people living anywhere else. The majority Burmans and the many minorities have a complicated culture, foreign and fascinating.

EDUCATION

About 85 percent of all children now spend four years or more in school. These years are usually from ages five to nine. The Burmese learn to read and write, do simple arithmetic, and are taught geography and history. Most schools are public, though there are still a few Buddhist schools, with monks as teachers, in rural areas. Buddhist schools also teach religion, primarily by memorization. *Kyaung* is the Burmese word for both monastery and school—that's an indication of where children have historically been taught.

There is one public schoolteacher for every twenty students. After kindergarten and the four years of school, a few children take tests to attend four years of middle school, then four years of high school. A very small number of Burmese are able to attend two-year technical colleges, four-year colleges in Rangoon or Mandalay, or vocational or teacher-training schools.

A high school chemistry class

Only about two-thirds of the population can read. That is because many older people never attended school. In contrast a few elderly Burmese were very well educated when Britain ran Burma. They attended English-language schools in Burma or Great Britain. These English-school graduates are often the sons and daughters of middle-class Burmese who worked in what the British called the Burma Civil Service. Now elderly, this group of people looks like everyone else in a town but still acts somewhat British at home.

OLD AGE BRINGS RESPECT

There are advantages to being old: age is respected and grandfathers and grandmothers at a meal with the family are served first. In return for such respect, grandparents give generous gifts when their grandchildren marry. Many also devote long

There is one public schoolteacher for every twenty students.

hours to their religion, whether in meditation at a temple, in giving to maintain the local pagoda, or in nat worship. Nats, or angels, allow Burmese to pray—Buddha isn't considered holy and Buddhism has no gods. The mother of the household usually cooks, makes cigars, preserves fruits and vegetables, keeps the huge water jar filled, and does crafts. The grandmother's job frequently is to place offerings of fruit or flowers each day in front of the tiny Buddhist altar found in almost every home.

Not many homes have indoor plumbing. But each village has a central well surrounded by a large wooden platform. Since the weather is almost always hot, villagers give themselves two or three baths a day on this platform. They do so modestly, moving their skirtlike longyis up and down their bodies to keep themselves covered.

Few homes have electricity, so batteries for radios are in short supply throughout the country.

The Burmese alphabet was devised by King Anawrahta in the eleventh century.

LANGUAGE

At least sixty-seven languages and dialects are spoken in Burma. The national language is Burmese and can be understood by about 80 percent of the population. Before independence, many Burmese spoke English as their second language. Today, Burmese most often hear English by listening to the British Broadcasting Corporation (BBC) news on short-wave radios. It remains the official second language, but the second language spoken by the country's minorities nowadays is Burmese. The people usually speak their own tongue at home and Burmese elsewhere.

Burmese is related to Tibetan. It is tonal like Chinese, which means that a simple sound such as "cha" can mean different things—to fall, a tiger, or a unit of money—depending on how it is pronounced. Punning—trading plays on words with friends—is a popular form of entertainment. The alphabet was devised by King Anawrahta in Pagan in the eleventh century from an Indian

The staples of Burmese cuisine are rice and fresh vegetables, readily available in open-air markets.

script. It looks like endless pieces of circles and resembles other Asian forms of writing, such as Khmer (in Cambodia) and Singhalese (in Sri Lanka).

FOOD

Burmese food is overshadowed by the famous menus of nearby China and India. Yet there are a number of original dishes, some more familiar than others. The standard meal centers around a generous helping of rice. This important grain is eaten with *ngapi*, a sharp-tasting and salty paste made from fermented fish or prawns. Clear, fish-flavored soup is included, as is a salad of raw green vegetables, plus a cooked vegetable dish, and a spicy curry or gravy that can contain pork, chicken, fish, or prawns. If visitors are being fed, more dishes will be added: oysters, turtle eggs, noodles, peas and beans, nuts, small cakes, fruits such as durians, pomelos, or pineapples, or various coconut-flavored items. Tea is the nation's most popular drink. Fruit juice and water-buffalo milk also are consumed.

Special occasions call for special foods. Rice, stuffed into sections of bamboo and cooked over an open fire, is eaten during holidays. So are such things as whole sparrows, oil from the heads of certain prawns, pastry, candy, sugarcane, gourds, and dozens of different tropical fruits. Meals often end with *lapet*, small bits of pickled tea leaves that taste like spicy spinach. The Burmese are a nation of snackers. Many of their favorite tidbits, such as lapet, are sold by vendors and are not made at home.

Some Burmese believe different foods have different effects on the diner. They consume fresh greens immediately after eating mushrooms, while a ginger-flavored salad must be eaten after dining on gooseberries. Many foods seem to have partners on the Burmese table. Meals are eaten without utensils and with the right hand. Following a meal, Burmese sometimes wrap a betel nut in a leaf with a smear of lime and chew it. Adults like the sharp taste, but they spit out the juice. Betel is a mild relaxer and stains the teeth of long-time users a deep maroon. Between meals, adult men and women smoke cheroots.

TRANSPORTATION

There are about fifty thousand cars and fifty thousand trucks in Burma. The cars are ancient, since there are no automobiles made in Burma and foreign cars that have been brought into the country since 1962 were purchased only by sailors and others earning money overseas. Ancient British, French, and American cars, kept running by inventive shade-tree mechanics, are used as taxis and run by the few families who can afford them. The trucks are a bit more modern: there are numerous Japanese pickups and

The trucks used in Burma tend to be a bit more up-to-date than the cars.

larger work trucks that haul wood, food, and other materials. Two-thirds of all roads are unpaved.

The trains run on rails 39 inches (1 meter) wide and are a popular way to travel from one city to another. There are 2,723 miles (4,382 kilometers) of rail line. Shorter trips are usually taken on ancient buses, frequently so overloaded that people ride atop them or stand on the rear bumpers. Neither trains nor buses are modern or comfortable. One visitor reported train tracks so bumpy that he had to cling to his train seat to avoid banging his head on the ceiling of the car. The rainy season often damages tracks and highways.

Two other forms of transportation show the difference between Burma and its more developed neighbors. The Irrawaddy River is navigable for 900 miles (1,448 kilometers) and is the country's most heavily traveled route of any kind. Ancient steamers and

The Irrawaddy River is Burma's most heavily traveled transportation route.

primitive rafts are common forms of transport. At the other
extreme, Rangoon's airport is visited by foreign commercial jets.
There are smaller airplanes that fly tourists between Rangoon,
Mandalay, Pagan, and Heho. Recently several Burma-owned
passenger planes have crashed, leading some governments to
advise their touring citizens against flying inside the country.

SPORTS AND RECREATION

Life isn't easy for the Burmese, so there is little time for
organized sports. Nevertheless, a game played with a *chinlon*, or
hollow wicker ball, is seen everywhere. The game is played by
keeping the ball in the air using feet, head, lower legs, and
knees—anything but the hands. The chinlon ball is sixteen inches
(forty centimeters) in diameter and the game is played by six
persons standing in a circle and passing the lightweight ball with
great skill.

Other popular sports include soccer, which uses the skills

Lunar Festival

learned in passing the chinlon, plus boxing, badminton, and other games familiar everywhere. Young children play with marbles, slingshots, seeds, and stones, while adults are heavy gamblers. Adults enjoy board games and astrology.

FESTIVALS

The Burmese look for excuses to hold festivals. Particularly in the dry season, freshly harvested fields all over the country become sites for markets, food vendors, sellers of arts and crafts, and more. There are pwes that can last for hours. Among the most unusual nationwide celebrations is the Water Festival. This three-day holiday takes place in April to celebrate the Burmese new year. Water is seen as washing away the old year. Consequently, people hurl buckets, jars, bowls, pots, and cups of water on each other. Perfect strangers are soaked and only monks and the elderly are off limits.

The Buddhist Lent is a three-month period of self-denial. Yet it is also a time of happy nat festivals, honoring one of thirty-seven angels left over from a religion practiced in Burma before Buddhism. Other festivals include Workers' Day in May, which also signals the start of the monsoon season, plus Independence Day in January, Union Day in February, and the Festival of Light in October. The latter holiday marks the end of Lent and is especially attractive. Lights blaze all across the country, illuminating fragile riverboats and huge pagodas alike. Although Christianity isn't common, December 25 is a public holiday too.

A MODERN BURMESE

Half of all Burmese are twenty years of age or younger. This is so because the birthrate is very high and life expectancy is only about fifty-two years of age for men and fifty-six years of age for women. There is only one hospital bed for every 1,539 Burmese,

Rangoon General Hospital

and just one doctor for every 4,467 citizens. Tuberculosis and hepatitis are common diseases, due to lack of sanitation.

Buddhist sabbath comes every eight days, but there are no regular services. Therefore, the days of the week seem much the same. People who live in the thousands of small villages work day in and day out when fields need tending and relax a bit during the weeks immediately after the harvest.

A typical Burmese, then, is about twenty years old, married at about the age of eighteen, and the parent of a child. He or she will eventually have four or more children. One of the four probably will either die at or shortly after birth, or before he or she reaches adulthood. Our typical Burmese has never used a telephone, never seen television, has heard, but does not own, a radio, and has never ridden in a car. Electricity can be found in his or her village, but few houses are wired for any kind of lights or appliances. Particularly if the person is a rural male, he will have several tattoos.

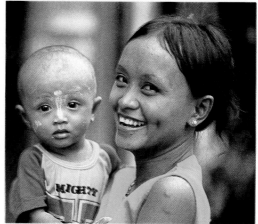

The faces of Burma

Ancient temples on the plain of Pagan

Living conditions are primitive. It is difficult to tell who is doing well and who is poor by the appearance of houses. Many urban homes have bars on the glassless windows to prevent entry by *dacoits*, roving gangs who break into homes. There is also the danger of occasional raids by bands of guerrilla soldiers.

Despite poverty and decades of bad government, the modern, young Burmese adult has a good understanding of religion, culture, and the history of the country. Recently, the country's residents have become much more politically active and aware. These days the economy makes it more difficult for them to pay their annual taxes to the village headman. Men and women have always been treated equally in legal matters and in ownership of property. Both try to live lives filled with good deeds, so that future lives will be even better.

MAP KEY

Allanmyo	E10
Andaman Sea	F9, F10, G9, G10
Arakan Ra. (mountain range)	E9
Athok	E10
Bassein	E9
Bengal, Bay of	D8, D9, E9, E10, F7, F8, F9, F10
Bhamo	D10
Bilin	E10
Bogale	E10
Chauk	D9
Cheduba I. (island)	E9
Chindwin (river)	C10, D9, D10
Gangaw	D9
Henzada	E10
Hkakabo Razi (mountain)	C10
Homalin	D9
Indaw	D10
Insein	E10
Irrawaddy (river)	C10, D10, D9, E10
Kalewa	D9
Kemaing	C10
Katha	D10
Kawthaung	F10
Keng Tung	D10
Kyaiklat	E10
Kyaukpyu	E9
Kyaukse	D10
Lashio	D10
Letpadan	E10
Lonkin	C10
Magwe	D9
Maliwun	F10
Mandalay	D10
Martaban	E10
Martaban, Gulf of	E10
Maungdaw	D9
Mawlaik	D9
Maymyo	D10
Meiktila	D10
Mergui	F10
Mergui Archipelago (islands)	F10
Minbu	D9
Mogok	D10
Mong Mitt	D10
Monywa	D10
Moscos Is. (islands)	F10
Moulmein	E10
Mouths of the Irrawaddy (river mouths)	E9, E10
Mudon	E10
Myingyan	D10
Myitkyina	C10
Naga Hills (mountains)	C10
Pagoda Point	E9
Pakokku	D9, D10
Paletwa	D9
Pangsau Pass	C10
Papun	E10
Pauk	D9
Paungde	E10
Pegu	E10
Prome	E10
Putao	C10
Pyapon	E10
Pyinmana	E10
Pyu	E10
Rangoon	E10
Sagaing	D10
Salween (river)	D10, E10
Sandoway	E9
Saw	D9
Shingbwiyang	C10
Shwebo	D10
Sittang (stream)	E10
Sittwe	D9
Taungdwingy	D10, E10
Taunggyi	D10
Tavoy	F10
Tenasserim	F10
Tharrawaddy	E10
Thaton	E10
Toungoo	E10
Victoria, Mt. (mountain)	D9
Wuntho	D10
Yamethin	D10
Ye	E10

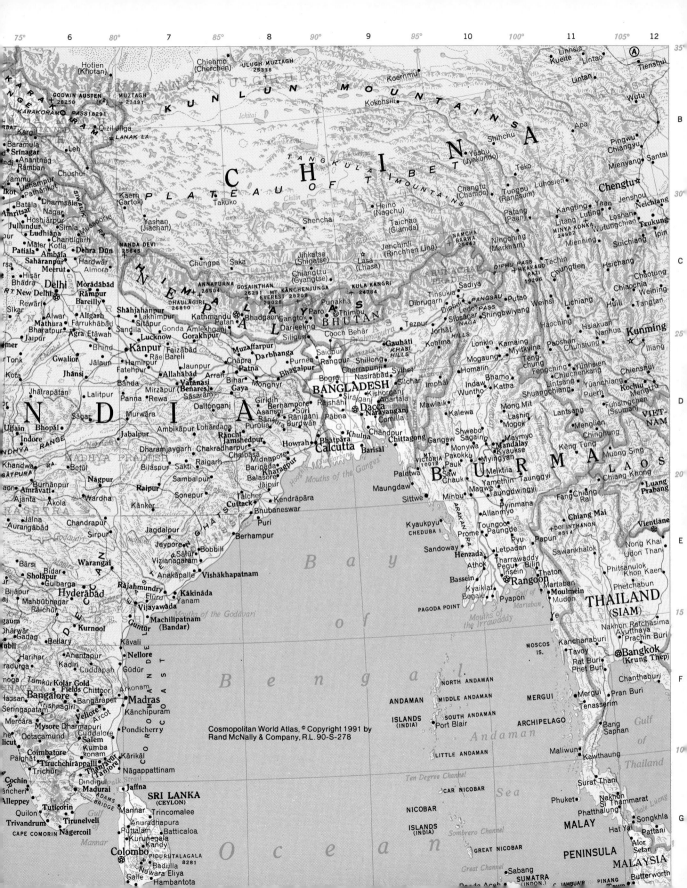

MINI-FACTS AT A GLANCE

GENERAL INFORMATION

Official Name: Myanma Nainggandaw (Republic of Burma). In 1989 the government in power changed the name to Union of Myanmar.

Capital: Rangoon, called Yangon by the Burmese

Official Language: Burmese. At least sixty-seven languages and dialects are spoken. During the colonial period English became the official language, and an elementary knowledge of English is still advantageous.

Government: Since September 1988 the country has been governed by a military junta known as the State Law and Order Restoration Council. There is universal suffrage for those eighteen years of age and older.

National Anthem: "Kaba Makye" ("Our Free Homeland")

Flag: A red field with dark blue in the upper left-hand corner, in which the state emblem in white, surrounded by 14 white stars, is featured.

Money: The basic unit of currency is the kyat. In December 1990, one Burmese kyat equaled $.1687 in U.S. currency.

Weights and Measures: Burma uses the metric system.

Population: 35,313,905 (1983 census)

Major Cities:
Rangoon	2,458,712
Mandalay	532,285
Moulmein	219,851
Pegu	150,447
Bassein	144,092

(Population figures based on 1983 census.)

Religion: Buddhism is the religion of almost all Burmese, though there are small numbers of Muslims, Christians, and Hindus.

Opposite page: Decorating laquerware

GEOGRAPHY

Highest Point: Hkakabo Razi, 19,296 ft. (5,881 m)

Lowest Point: Sea level

Mountains: Burma is very mountainous in the north and west. The northern mountains are made up of ranges reaching almost 20,000 ft. (6,096 m). The western ranges are lower in height, rising from 6,000 to 10,000 ft. (1,829 to 3,048 m). They form the border with India.

Rivers: Major rivers begin in northern Burma or southern China. The Irrawaddy, the Salwean, and the Sittang have been transportation routes for centuries. The Irrawaddy is navigable for 900 mi. (1,448 km).

Climate: Monsoons, or rain-bearing winds, sweep across Burma and create three seasons: the rainy season, from May to October; a cool and dry season, from October to February; and the hot, dry season from March to May. The eastern coastal regions and mountains receive about 200 in. (500 cm) of rain a year, whereas the rain in the delta and plains rarely exceeds 100 in. (254 cm). The average temperature is 81° F. (27° C). On the plains near Mandalay temperatures can exceed 100° F. (37.7° C).

Greatest Distances: North to south—1,300 mi. (2,090 km)
East to west—580 mi. (930 km)

Area: 261,218 mi.² (676,552 km²)

NATURE

Trees: Forests of bamboo or hardwoods, plus palm or pine, grow thickly. Teak is one of the most valuable. In the Irrawaddy and Sittang deltas there are mangrove trees that supply firewood, charcoal, and bark for tanning. Sandalwood trees provide wood for furniture and an oil used for perfume.

Animals: Elephants, tigers, leopards, and wild cats are common; bears are found in hilly regions, monkeys in the forest, and snakes of all kinds and crocodiles inhabit the river deltas. Rhinoceroses, wild buffalo, bison, and deer are scarce and must be protected. Tiny, silent lizards, called geckos, are found everywhere.

Fish: Fish are numerous and are found in streams, rice paddies, and in the ocean. Freshwater European carp and catfish are plentiful, as are more exotic fish like saltwater tiger prawns (shrimp) or squid.

Birds: Pheasants, parrots, peacocks, wild fowl, and grouse are prevalent, especially during the rainy seasons in the tropical jungles.

EVERYDAY LIFE

Food: Rice is the most important element in the Burmese diet. Fish is the next and it is eaten fresh, preserved, or made into a paste called *ngapi* and eaten with rice. Fish-flavored soup, salad, a cooked vegetable dish, and a curry made from pork, chicken, fish, or prawns compete a meal. Tea is the most popular drink. The Burmese enjoy snacks; some of their favorite things to eat are bought from street vendors.

Housing: Villagers live in wooden houses with bamboo walls and thatch roofs. There is no electricity and heat comes from a small central fireplace on a front porch where food is cooked.

Holidays

January 4, Independence Day
February 12, Union Day
March 27, Resistance Day
April 17, New Year's Day
May 1, Workers' Day
May 2, Burma Peasants' Day
July 19, Martyrs' Day
November 25, National Day
December 25, Christmas Day

Culture: Buddhism has pervaded Burmese life since the eleventh century and has blended with folk culture. Examples of religious architecture are visible throughout the country.

Drama, dance, and music combine to create *pwes*, a distinctive kind of theater seen at Burmese festivals. The Burmese National Theater has traveled around the world. The cinema is popular as are traditional and modern musical performances on TV.

Woodcarving, lacquer and work in gold and silver metals depict Buddhist images and mythological figures. Bronze and brass sculpture, embroidery, furniture, jewelry, knitwear, marble sculpture, metalwork, umbrellas, and weaving are outstanding Burmese crafts. The ministry of culture is working hard to revive and sustain these indigenous arts.

Sports and Recreation: The Burmese enjoy such organized sports as soccer and boxing. A game using a *chinlon*, or hollow wicker ball, is played everywhere. Children play with marbles, slingshots, seeds, and stones. Adults enjoy gambling, board games, and astrology.

Communication: Mass communication is operated by the government. There is one newspaper published in both a Burmese and an English edition and one TV channel.

Transportation: The Irrawaddy River is the main avenue of commercial transport. Trade in rice is carried on over smaller navigable rivers as well. The first railway line, built in 1877, followed the Irrawaddy Valley. The Rangoon-Mandalay-Myitkyina railway is now the main artery. Two-thirds of all roads are unpaved. The Union of Burma Airways runs domestic and international flights. Small planes fly between Rangoon, Mandalay, Pegu, and Heho. Tourist flights to the ancient capital of Pagan are a major source of foreign currency.

Education: The literacy rate in Burma had always been high, and continues to improve. Education is free and required between the ages of five and nine, and there are only nominal fees for secondary schools and universities. There are still a few Buddhist schools in rural areas. Universities are located at Rangoon and Mandalay. There are also four degree-granting colleges, three institutes of medicine, and institutes of dentistry, veterinary science, economics, technology, education, and foreign languages. Most post-secondary educational institutions have been closed since the 1988 rebellion.

Health: The infant mortality rate has been lowered and health units have been expanded into villages.

ECONOMY AND INDUSTRY

Chief Products:
Agriculture: Rice, sugarcane, chilies, sesame seeds, wheat, tea, coffee, strawberries, peanuts, beans, corn, tobacco, rubber, cotton, jute
Forestry: Teak
Manufacturing: Fertilizer, processed foods
Mining: Rubies, jade, sapphires, emeralds, pearls, petroleum, natural gas, antimony, coal, zinc, lead, tin, tungsten, silver, gypsum, limestone

IMPORTANT DATES

3rd century, B.C.—The Mons come from southern China to live in southeast Burma

About A.D. 100—Tibeto-Burmans occupy much of northern and central Burma

6th century—Burmans take over cities and the Shan tribe moves in from what is now Thailand

825—Mon capital founded in Pegu

849—Burman capital, Pagan, is built

1044—King Anawrahta assumes the throne, encourages Theravada Buddhism, develops written Burmese language and translation of Buddhist works; beginning of the Pagan Dynasty

1287—Kublai Khan's Mongol hordes invade and destroy the political order, ending the Pagan Dynasty; death of Marathihapate

1519—Portuguese begin trading in Southeast Asia

1546—Tabinshwehti crowned king of all Burma

1599—Philip de Brito, a Portuguese sailor, declares himself king in Syriam for 14 years

1600s—British, Dutch, and French companies trade with the Burmese

1752—Country is reunited under King Alaungpaya

1766—Chinese attempt to invade Burma but are driven back

1824-86—Burma annexed to British India in three Anglo-Burmese Wars

1853—King Mindon becomes ruler of Burma, until 1878

1857—Mandalay becomes capital

1872—Fifth Great Synod of Buddhism

1878—Thibaw, who was anti-British, becomes king, until 1885

1935—Burma is separated from India

1942—Japanese conquer Burma

1945—Japanese defeated

1947—Anti-Fascist People's Freedom League (AFPFL), headed by Aung San, received a majority of votes when a constituent assembly is formed; constituent assembly calls for independence; Aung San is assassinated

1948—Burma becomes a fully independent nation outside the Commonwealth under U Nu. Long guerrilla war begins

1962—General Ne Win leads coup d'etat and strives to make Burma a socialist state

1988—Monks and students stage protest against government; Ne Win steps down; General Saw Maung takes control as head of State Law and Order Restoration Council

1989—Government in power changes country's name to Union of Myanmar

1990—The National League for Democracy party headed by Aung San Suu Kyi, opposing army rule, wins election by a landslide, but leadership is arrested

IMPORTANT PEOPLE

King Alaungpaya (1711-60), reunited country in 1752; repelled Chinese invasion

King Anaukhpethlun of Toungoo (?-1629), led army against Philip de Brito in 1613 and defeated him

King Anawrahta, reigned 1044-77; unified upper and lower Burma

Aung San Suu Kyi (1945-   ), daughter of Aung San, well educated contemporary leader opposed to military government

King Bagyidaw, was cause of First Anglo-Burmese War in 1824

Philip de Brito (?-1613), Portuguese sailor; declared himself king of lower Burma but was deposed in 1613

Kublai Khan (1216-94), head of the Mongol armies that overtook Burma in 13th century

King Mindon (1814-78), became ruler of Burma in 1853; held Fifth Great Synod of Buddhism in 1872

Narathihapate, last king before Mongol invasion, ruled from 1254-87

General Ne Win (1911-   ), took over government 1962; collapse of his Socialist economy and his official resignation led to rebellion of 1988

U Nu (1907-   ), prime minister from 1948-62; president AFPFL (Anti-Fascist People's Freedom League)

Khun Sa (Chang Chi-fu), leader of the trade in opium; tried to make a deal with United States to stop exporting heroin in return for a payoff

General Aung San (1915-47), wartime and postwar hero; founded AFPFL

General Saw Maung (1928-   ), took power in September 1988

Tabinshwehti (1512-50), crowned king of all Burma in 1546

Thibaw (1858-1916), last king of Burma; exiled by the British

INDEX

Page numbers that appear in boldface type indicate illustrations

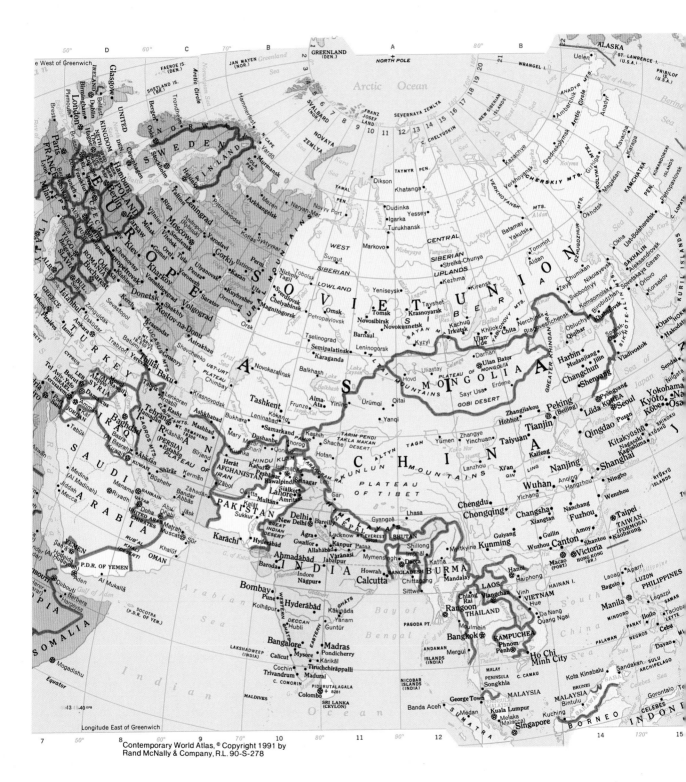

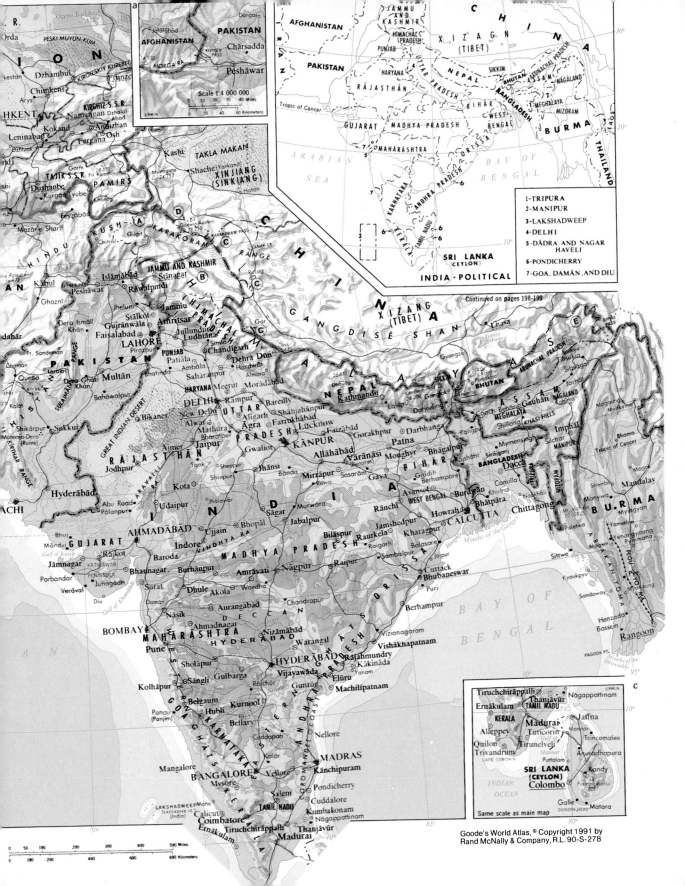

INDIA - POLITICAL

1-TRIPURA
2-MANIPUR
3-LAKSHADWEEP
4-DELHI
5-DĀDRA AND NAGAR HAVELI
6-PONDICHERRY
7-GOA, DAMĀN, AND DIU

Continued on pages 198–199

Goode's World Atlas, © Copyright 1991 by
Rand McNally & Company, R.L. 90-S-278

About the Author

David Wright was born and grew up in Richmond, Indiana. He first visited Asia while serving in the U.S. army in Vietnam. Wright has spent more than ten years in newspapers as a reporter, copy editor, and editor. Newspapers range from *The Chicago Tribune* to *The Monroe* (Wisconsin) *Evening Times*.

Wright has written these books in the Enchantment of the World series: *Brunei*, *Malaysia*, and *Vietnam*. He has written five other books for Childrens Press, including the four-book series, *War in Vietnam*. He has written several books for adults.

He and his wife and two children live in West Bend, Wisconsin, 40 miles northwest of Milwaukee. He has been a fulltime freelance writer, editor, and photographer for ten years.